Current Topics in Technology:
Social, Legal, Ethical, and
Industry Issues for Computers
and
the Internet

Maureen Sheehan Paparella

Eugene Simko

THOMSON

COURSE TECHNOLOGY

Australia • Canada • Mexico • Singapore • Spain • United Kingdom • United States

Current Topics in Technology: Social, Legal, Ethical, and Industry Issues for Computers and the Internet

Maureen Sheehan Paparella

Eugene Simko

Executive Editor:
Alexandra Arnold

Marketing Manager:
Joy Stark-Vancs

Product Manager:
Heather Hawkins

Editorial Assistant:
Jon Farnham

Content Project Manager:
Matt Hutchinson

Cover Designer:
Kathleen Fivel

Manufacturing Coordinator:
Julio Esperas

Compositor:
GEX Publishing Services

Printer:
Globus

CURRENT TOPICS IN TECHNOLOGY
Contents

PREFACE

Learning Goals and Objectives

Traditional information technology courses stress the mechanics of "how things work" within a fundamental conceptual framework, both on the computer and across the ether of the Internet. The supplemental use of current technology topics, as covered in various media, will "bring alive" subject matter addressed within the curricula and provide a higher level of course satisfaction by students.

This compilation of *Current Topics in Technology* is designed to elevate courses in technology to challenge and divert students to develop a higher level cognitive ability that will parallel social, legal, and ethical awareness in the study of technology. Students are guided through a wealth of topics that provide insight into the crucial role that technology occupies in both the personal and professional lives of managers of all organizations. Students will explore their role and responsibilities to the environment and society to ensure that productivity and technical risks are appropriately managed, preparing students for the challenges of leadership. The systematic exercise of the perusal, analysis, and recitation of multiple topics throughout the course will compel students to pursue the content and edification of future topics autonomously. When utilized as part of the critical methods of instruction in introductory courses, the literature and exercises have proven to inspire a greater interest in technology education.

Critical Pedagogy

Students are provided an article overview that serves to introduce the technology topic, providing key background information, which will provide the social, historical, or antecedent events necessary to understand the topic. Following the article, critical thinking questions are provided to stimulate intellectual discussions regarding particular social, political, and ethical values, such as privacy, ownership, crime, responsibility and risk, while concomitantly reinforcing technical concepts.

Most topics are approached as a mini-case study, similar in approach to the Harvard Business School's practice of detailing an account of a real-life situation in which a dilemma that takes place in a real-life organization is described. This material is utilized most effectively when students read the article and complete the answers to questions individually in writing before meeting in collaborative teams, utilizing the campus extranet system for use of the asynchronous discussion board. Students are motivated by the contrasting perspectives and analyses they share with each other. Following this segue, the discussion is approached in the physical or electronic classroom, using the instructor as the facilitator of the forum. Finally, students are encouraged to participate in scholarly research on topics that emanate from this discussion.

Acknowledgements

The authors extend their appreciation to the Information Technology students of Monmouth University, and members of the Software Engineering Department and School of Business Administration faculty at Monmouth University, for their role in inspiring this effort. Many members of the Information Technology faculty, in particular, made numerous recommendations for articles of interest. Students and faculty provided both anecdotal and survey responses, supporting the value of this modality in our pedagogy. Students and faculty provided the commitment and fervor that stimulated this response.

About the Authors

Maureen Sheehan Paparella and Gene Simko have collaborated on a multitude of research efforts over the last decade, in technology education and management of information systems. Their most recent research interests have included the implementation of SWOT analysis for technical management in government, serving as consultants to the Federal Bureau of Investigation at Fort Monmouth, New Jersey, and at headquarters in Washington, D.C. in 2005.

Maureen Sheehan Paparella earned a BA degree, magna cum laude, from St. Thomas University, Miami, Florida, and earned a MBA from Barry University, Miami, Florida, where she later taught undergraduate and graduate courses in computer programming and developed new curricula in accounting information systems. As a pioneer in the microcomputer industry, Professor Paparella was a software trainer for Texas Instruments, Inc.; she served as the Coordinator for Microcomputer Product Support for South Florida, supervising a staff of management trainers, developing technical training programs and conducting research for the Consumer Products Division, and directing technology educational programs for the Education Division. She also served as the General Manager of a dealership that served the computing needs of the South Florida legal market for Sony Corporation of America. Professor Paparella joined the faculty of the Computer Science Department at Monmouth University in 1994, and was appointed Director of Information Technology for the Software Engineering Department in 1997, where she has authored and implemented an Information Technology Minor and Certificate Program, specifically designed for non-technology majors, and a Teacher Computer Camp for K-12 educators. In 2003, she received the Stafford Award for Administrative Excellence. In 2006, she was appointed to the Board of Directors of the International Council on Innovative Higher Education.

Eugene Simko attended the United States Military Academy at West Point, earned a BS degree and MBA degree from Temple University, Philadelphia, Pennsylvania, and a Doctorate of Strategic Management from Baruch College of the City University of New York. Dr. Simko has consulted for a wide array of organizations in both the public and private sectors, including AT&T, Ralston Purina, Northern Telecom, National Association of Purchasing Managers, Reed Jewelers, Tethered Communications, Bell Northern Research, Mitel, New Jersey Natural Gas, and the American Management Association. He recently served as Acting President of the International Council of Innovative Higher Education. Dr. Simko is a commissioned officer in the U.S. Army Reserves; served on the New Jersey Assembly Task Force on Business Retention, Expansion and Export Opportunities; and was appointed by the Governor of New Jersey to the New Jersey Battleship Commission. Dr. Simko is a member of the graduate faculty of the Department of Management and Marketing at Monmouth University, has served in numerous administrative posts, such as Associate Provost, Director of Graduate Studies, Director of the MBA program, and Vice President of the Faculty Association. Dr. Simko is a recipient of the Monmouth University Distinguished Teaching Award.

FORUM 1

Safeguarding Against Cyber Terrorism

Article Overview

Terrorism is now deemed a major threat to vital information networks worldwide. In the development of a system for safeguarding these networks in the United States, the Department of Homeland Security developed an administrative post in 2003. In the three years for which this post has been filled, three individuals have resigned and tests of the measures in place have failed. How can government begin to develop an effective system to control cyber terrorism?

Article: *Top Cyber-Security Post Is Filled*

By BRIAN KREBS
Monday, September 18, 2006 6:40 PM
WashingtonPost.com

The Department of Homeland Security on Monday announced that a technology industry lobbyist will become the nation's top cyber-security official, filling a key post that has been vacant since Congress created the position more than 14 months ago.

Greg Garcia, the vice president of information security policy and programs for the Information Technology Association of America, will become the first-ever assistant secretary for cyber-security and telecommunications.

In a written statement, DHS Secretary Michael Chertoff said "Greg brings the right mix of experience in government and the private sector to continue to strengthen our robust partnerships that are essential to this field." Garcia did not return calls seeking comment.

Garcia will oversee DHS's implementation of the "National Strategy to Secure Cyberspace," a far-reaching blueprint for securing the nation's most critical information networks and for crafting a disaster-recovery and response plan in case of a major cyber-attack or other massive malfunction.

The strategy, first released in early 2003, envisions strong industry and government collaboration should an attack or malfunction disrupt the information systems that control the most vital information networks — such as those that control regional telecommunications, water and power systems.

Insufficient progress has been made in meeting those goals over the past three years, according to a DHS report released last week summarizing the results of "Cyber Storm," a four-day exercise designed to test how nimbly industry and the government would respond to a concerted cyber attack on key information systems. The report suggested that government and private-sector participants had trouble recognizing the coordinated attacks, determining whom to contact, and organizing a response.

"I think Cyber Storm showed that we really haven't made that much progress in figuring out how we'd respond if something bad like this does happen," said James Lewis, director of technology and public policy at the Center for Strategic and International Studies, a think tank located in Washington, D.C. "With just two and a half years left, this administration is on a tight timeline to get anything done here.... But Greg is a great pick and should be able get things up and running at a good pace."

Past candidates for the post have been criticized by industry groups either for not having enough clout in Washington or not enough experience in the private sector. Garcia's experience in both worlds — he served several years as a congressional staffer and as head of the Washington office for 3Com Corp., a Santa Clara, Calif.-based networking equipment company — makes him an ideal choice for the job, said Shannon Kellogg, director of government and industry affairs at RSA, the security division of EMC Corp.

"He's a solid choice and will do a good job," Kellogg. "At the same time, it's important for him not to go in there and try to boil the ocean. He needs to choose three or four key priorities on cyber and work to move those forward."

The DHS cyber-security post was originally assigned to a lower hierarchical rung when the agency was first created in 2003. Three former top cyber-security officials resigned, and two complained publicly about their lack of authority, prompting Congress to elevate the position to the assistant secretary role last year.

Things to Think About

1. What is the purpose of the new position of Assistant Secretary for Cyber-Security and Telecommunications? What prompted Congress to elevate the post from its original hierarchical rung at the Department of Homeland Security?

2. What are your thoughts regarding the criticisms of those who held the position in the past? How would you defend them? What strengths does Greg Garcia bring to the position that might overcome those criticisms?

3. Is the national strategy appropriate? Do you agree with the determination made as to the most vital information networks? What other information networks would you include on that list?

4. Name an event in history that is reminiscent of the outcome of the CyberStorm exercise. Explain.

5. Why does Kellogg suggest that Garcia limit his priorities? Is it possible for Garcia to meet the administration's timeline?

Key Terms

1. CyberStorm

2. National Strategy to Secure Cyberspace

FORUM 2

Digitization and Copyright Law

Article Overview

Sergey Brin and Larry Page tell an altruistic story of a dream to digitize *all* the world's books, both public domain and copyrighted. Adversaries believe their ambition is part of a skillful strategy of increased market share for Google. Now billionaires, just eight years after a startup operation out of a rented garage, they are more determined than ever to achieve this goal. What challenges do they face?

Article: *Search Me?: Google Wants to Digitize Every Book: Publishers Say Read the Fine Print First*

By BOB THOMPSON
August 13, 2006
The Washington Post; p. D01

STANFORD, Calif. Google Wants to Digitize Every Book. Publishers Say Read the Fine Print First. If it is really true that Google is going to digitize the roughly 9 million books in the libraries of Stanford University, then you can be sure that the folks who brought you the world's most ambitious search engine will come, in due time, for call number E169 D3.

Google workers will pull Lillian Dean's 1950 travelogue "This Is Our Land" — the story of one family's "pleasant and soul-satisfying auto journey across our continent" — from a shelf in the second-floor stacks of the Cecil H. Green Library. They will place the slim blue volume on a book cart, wheel it into a Google truck backed up to the library's loading dock and whisk it a few miles southeast to the Googleplex, the $100 billion-plus company's sprawling, campuslike headquarters in Mountain View. There, at an undisclosed location, it will be scanned and added to the ever-expanding universe of digitally searchable knowledge.

Why undisclosed?

Because for one thing, in their race to assemble the greatest digital library the world has ever seen, Google's engineers have developed sophisticated technology they'd prefer their competitors not see.

And for another, perhaps — though Google executives don't say so directly — the library scanning program already has generated a *little* too much heat.

Last fall, the Authors Guild and a group of major publishing houses filed separate suits in U.S. District Court in Manhattan, charging Google with copyright infringement on a massive scale. Google argues that under the "fair use" provisions of copyright law, it has a perfect right to let its users search the text of copyrighted works — as long as, once the search is complete, it only shows them what it calls "snippets" of those works. Nonsense, say the authors and publishers: In order to find and display those snippets, Google must first copy whole books without permission.

Books like E169 D3 — which finds itself smack at the heart of this contested legal territory.

"Great example," says Andrew Herkovic, the communications and development director for Stanford's libraries, as he pauses to consider "This Is Our Land" during a Green Library tour.

There's a 10-1 chance, Herkovic estimates, that its copyright expired without being renewed, which would put it safely in the public domain.

But "if you were the corporate counsel for Stanford, Google or anybody else, is 10 to 1 good enough?"

California Dreamin'

To travel to Silicon Valley and consider the fate of E169 D3 — along with the tens of millions of other volumes Google hopes to scan, from Stanford and a number of other major libraries — is to open a window on the future of books in the digital age.

It's also to be swept up in the saga of Google itself: the seat-of-the-pants enterprise that computer science whizzes Sergey Brin and Larry Page moved out of their cramped quarters at Stanford in 1998 — just eight years ago! — and into Susan Wojcicki's garage.

Silicon Valley cliche to the contrary, Wojcicki — who was a friend of a friend of Brin's with a new house and mortgage worries — says she rented them more than just a garage. "They had the garage and three bedrooms and two bathrooms," she recalls, confirming and clarifying the Legend of the Google Guys. "Yes, they stored stuff in the garage and they had servers and they had meetings. But it was winter, so it was actually kind of cold."

Laughing, she continues:

"The washing machine was in the garage, too. That was considered a key asset at the time."

Wojcicki is now the company's vice president for product management. As such, she's been involved in the book-scanning project for years. She's talking, on this blue-sky California day, in a small conference room crammed with colorful beanbag chairs. Outside, the lunchtime barbecue is over — Google is famous for its perpetually free food — and people zip from building to building on bright yellow motorized scooters.

Digitizing all the world's books "was an idea of Sergey and Larry's from very early on," Wojcicki says. In fact, they were supposed to be working on a small library digitization project "when they wound up creating a search engine, which today we know as Google."

Brin and Page tried to "monetize" their brainchild by peddling it to established Internet companies. When that didn't work, they switched to an advertising strategy — but one that differed fundamentally from most Web advertising at the time. Rather than intrusive banner ads or pop-ups, the pair went with text-only advertising tied to the key words Google searchers typed in.

Worked like a charm. In the summer of 2004, Google went public and the Google Guys became instant multibillionaires. Google employees and investors (Stanford prominent among them) got a lot richer as well.

You'd think building a company that "may supplant Microsoft as the most important — and most profitable — corporation ever created" (as journalist John Battelle put it in his 2005 book "The Search") would have kept the pair busy enough. But no: According to Wojcicki, they never lost sight of their digital library dream.

She first heard them talk about it in early 2000, when "we didn't have the resources even to do our core business." But Brin and Page did more than just talk, even then:

"They actually would do some of the math behind it," Wojcicki says, "and calculate, like, how many machines it would take, how many hours it would take. So they knew with certain assumptions that it was a doable project."

It got more doable as the bucks started pouring in.

Brin and Page set a team of engineers to work on scanning technology. Later, they asked Wojcicki and her people to start acquiring books to scan. The first move was to negotiate with publishers for access to their current books.

Product manager Adam Smith explains how these deals work. With the publisher's permission, Google scans the full texts and makes the books searchable by key word. Users can't download a whole book, Smith says, but they can see sample pages — "publishers can set a dial in terms of how much" — and Google offers links to sites where the books can be purchased.

"The partner program is really an online marketing tool to help publishers," says content partnerships director Jim Gerber, who works with Smith and Wojcicki. Most major houses have signed on.

So far, so good.

But as Googlers will tell you, over and over, the goal of Google Book Search — the current name for the overall scanning program — is "to create a comprehensive, full-text searchable database of all the world's books."

Not some. All.

"We're Google. We like doing things at scale," as Wojcicki puts it.

Problem was, fewer than 5 percent of "all the world's books" were in print and available from Google's publishing partners.

So where were the *rest* of them going to come from?

'The Final Encyclopedia'

Sometime in 2002, Stanford's head librarian, Michael Keller, got an invitation to an exclusive gathering that would change his professional life.

The host was Microsoft billionaire Paul Allen. The location was Allen's place in the San Juan Islands, near Seattle, where a dozen or so high-level information technologists convened with an agenda that grew out of Allen's fascination with a science fiction novel called "The Final Encyclopedia."

"You know that novel? Gordon Dickson?" Keller asks. "It informed Paul's thinking. His question was: Are we near the point where we can have *every* piece of information, every fact, every record of every opinion and attitude, every bit of criticism, all the history of all the world's decisions and so forth . . . in one giant database?"

Google's Page had been invited to the San Juans, too. He and Keller talked. In September 2003, Keller and Herkovic drove down to Mountain View to hear a proposition from Page and some other Googlers.

"It was a very short conversation," Keller says. "Basically they said, 'What do you think about digitizing every book in the library?' And we said, 'Yay!' "

Stanford's librarian scarcely needed convincing about what digitization could do. After the university digitized its card catalogue, he says, use of the collection jumped 50 percent — simply because books were easier to find. Another successful Stanford venture, HighWire Press, offers access to digitized scholarly journal articles.

Meanwhile, the library has been scanning books itself for decades. A few years ago, it bought a Swiss-made robotic scanner and set it to work in the Green basement. With 50 such robots, Keller calculated — at a capital cost of something like $75 million — the university could digitize its library all by itself. He got a few foundations interested, but they backed off.

Small wonder that when the Google offer came along, Keller jumped at it.

Not without a *lot* of due diligence, however, mostly about the legality of including books like call number E169 D3.

"Copyright 1950, Vantage Press, Inc. All Rights Reserved" reads the notice in "This Is Our Land" — a clear enough warning at the time, but what does it mean, more than half a century later? The book is not in print, a fact that is easily ascertained. But does Vantage Press even still exist? Was the copyright ever renewed, and if so, who owns it now: the publisher, the author or the author's heirs? These questions are not so easily answered.

Most important, perhaps, even assuming Dean's book *is* still under copyright, would it be "fair use" for Google to copy it anyway, allowing it to be searched but making only "snippets" of text available for public view? (Fair use is a section of U.S. copyright law that allows portions of a work to be reproduced without permission under certain circumstances — for example, in criticism, news reporting and scholarship.)

Keller asked Stanford's general counsel to help him consider this question. He consulted Stanford law professors and outside copyright experts, too. "We end up having a big seance," he says. "We get lots of opinions."

He makes no bones about what he was really after. Having his library included in Google's searchable database will be a fine thing, he says, but the real benefit to Stanford will come from the newly digitized copies of its own books that the university will receive from Google as a quid pro quo.

Keller starts ticking off the reasons they'll be so important. One is preservation. "We don't have enough invested in this country," he says, "to assure that printed materials are going to persist." Another is the potential for truly complex search. There are far more sophisticated ways than Google's key word approach through which the library can help its users mine data.

A fully digitized library, Keller enthuses, will be an unbelievable new intellectual resource: a "test bed" in which everyone from anthropologists to zoologists can experiment with varieties of research impossible to imagine before.

Why not go for it?

When Google announced the library scanning project, in December 2004, it had four library partners besides Stanford. Two of them (Oxford University and the New York Public Library) took a legally cautious approach to digitization, permitting Google to copy only public domain works. A third, the University of Michigan, took the opposite view, asserting forcefully that Google could scan every one of its 7 million books. Harvard hedged its bets, initially agreeing only to a limited test program. Last week, the University of California signed on as a sixth Google partner. Its scanning program will include both public domain and copyrighted material.

Stanford, despite Keller's enthusiasm, is still hedging a bit. The librarian believes that scanning even in-print books would be legal. For the time being, however — because who knows when those lawsuits will be resolved — only out-of-print material is getting trucked down to Mountain View.

"But you've *got* to hear me talk about those two suits," Keller says. "I can't wait for them to come up."

He proceeds to explain, vehemently and at some length, why Google's use of copyrighted work is "transformative" (part of the legal definition of fair use) and why search doesn't hurt the marketplace for a book (another fair use criterion).

"Transforming all the words in the book into a giant index is wrong somehow? Give me a break," he says. "And someone's going to get paid for that? Give me a *bigger* break."

But getting paid is what it comes down to, he thinks — and the lawsuits are a way to force the issue.

"If you look at what the publishers are asking," Keller says, "I think they're trying to get Google to negotiate."

Permission, Permission

If Allan Adler were in the same room with Keller, he'd likely be saying: Of course publishers want to negotiate! The whole problem is that Google won't!

Instead, the vice president for legal and government affairs for the Association of American Publishers sits in the trade association's offices at the foot of Capitol Hill, shaking his head at what he sees as the breathtaking arrogance of it all.

"In order to provide online searchability," Adler says, Google has to create "a proprietary database that in essence would be the world's largest digital library." Extremely impressive, way cool — and clearly of enormous value, or the company wouldn't be spending so much to do it.

From New York, Authors Guild Executive Director Paul Aiken echoes Adler's incredulity. "It's an attempt to avoid licensing," Aiken says. "Without the ability to say no, a rights holder really has nothing to license."

All together now: *What part of "we own the copyright" doesn't Google understand?*

The Googlers certainly seemed to understand it, Adler says, when they negotiated with publishers for the right to copy and search their in-print books. Both sides were happy with *that* part of the Book Search program, which Google announced in October 2004.

Just two months later, the company announced its library deals.

It took a while for the publishers to react. Individual houses talked to Google, but it wasn't until the spring that they got concerned enough collectively to ask their trade association to intervene. In July, at the AAP's New York headquarters, Adler and other publishing representatives met with Smith, Gerber and Google CEO Eric Schmidt. The focus, Adler says, was on what to do with the millions of noncurrent titles that are not yet in the public domain.

"We were essentially told, 'Look, this is a problem of scalability,' " Adler says. Google was going to be "backing up trucks" to collect books for scanning. How could it puzzle out copyright status book by book?

Three weeks *after* the meeting, Google surprised the publishers with a unilateral move. The company had always said it would respect an author or publisher's request to "opt out" of the Book Search program after a book was scanned. Now it would accept opt-out requests in advance. To facilitate this, it declared a three-month scanning moratorium.

No, no, no, said the publishers. We should be *in* control here: You need us to opt in.

On Sept. 20, 2005, the Authors Guild filed a class action suit against Google, seeking statutory damages and an injunction to halt the scanning. A month later, five major publishers — McGraw-Hill, Pearson Education, Penguin Group (USA), Simon & Schuster and John Wiley & Sons — sued as well, with the support of the AAP. The publishers didn't ask for damages because they didn't want the focus to be on money.

Permission, permission is their refrain.

Listen long enough to both sides in this dispute and your head will spin with legal citations and passionate argument. But it's possible to isolate key points of contention. Among them:

- Copyright and fair use: As Google's Gerber puts it, the two sides obviously have a "fundamental difference about what is required to build an index of information." Because whole books or even whole pages are not displayed, Gerber and his colleagues argue, making copyrighted books searchable is the kind of "transformative use" permitted under copyright law. The publishers and the Authors Guild completely disagree, arguing that Google's unlicensed creation and retention of digital copies — as well as its creation of additional copies for the libraries — are illegal.

- Money and motivation: "Google would like the world to see this as a purely altruistic act on its part," says the AAP's Adler. Instead, he argues, searchable books are part of the company's "very brilliant economic strategy" for differentiating itself from competitive search engines. If you're worried that Yahoo, Microsoft or some unknown startup will scoop up lucrative market share, adding books to your database helps you stay ahead.

Google executives downplay this analysis but don't deny it. "The reason we're doing it," Wojcicki says, is that "making Google more comprehensive will yield a better search experience." Yes, that should lead — eventually — to more users and more revenue. But Book Search, she cautions, also represents a huge outlay of capital and isn't guaranteed to pay off anytime soon. It's a risk, as Gerber points out, you don't see *publishers* lining up to take.

- The Web search analogy: This gets a bit complicated, but it's crucial to understanding the dispute over Google's library scanning. Wojcicki, Smith, Gerber and Google attorney Alexander Macgillivray — whom Smith calls "our thought leader" on intellectual property issues — all insist that there's very little difference between the basic functioning of their Web search engine and Book Search.

The comparison goes like this:

To index the Web, Google first sends out software programs called "crawlers" that explore the online universe, link by link, making copies of every site they find — just as Book Search makes a digital copy of every book it can lay its hands on. Web sites are protected by copyright, so if you don't *want* your site indexed by Google and its search brethren, you can "opt out," usually by employing a nifty technological watchdog (a file called robots.txt) that tells search engines to bug off.

Ditto for books, Google argues: Publishers and authors can opt out by informing Google that they don't want their books scanned and made searchable.

The analogy carries a risk for Google. Former Wired editor Kevin Kelly, one of the most influential journalists covering the digital revolution, sums it up this way: "If they capitulate on this with the publishers, they jeopardize their entire ability to search the Web."

Google executives don't sound worried. "No judge is going to rule that Web search is illegal," Macgillivray says. Still, they're on the horns of a dilemma. To use the Web analogy in court is on some level to bet the company, however favorable the odds.

No need to fret, say the publishers: The analogy fails in any case.

Most Web sites, they point out, are *designed* to be free. Books are not. As for the "opt out" requirement, as one high-ranking publishing executive explains it — he doesn't want to be named; odds are he'll be dealing with Google in the future — publishing houses have already installed a perfectly good, low-tech version of robots.txt.

"It's called a price," he says.

'Don't Be Evil'

Five years ago, Google's head of human resources rounded up a dozen or so early employees and asked them to try to identify the company's core values. As Battelle reports in "The Search," instead of the usual mush of corporate platitudes, a striking three-word slogan emerged: "Don't be evil."

As company mottos go, it was succinct, distinctive — and just a tiny bit hard to live up to.

Eight years after Page and Brin incorporated Google and took over Wojcicki's garage, the company still retains some of its don't-be-evil halo. It offers a wonderfully efficient, free tool now used by countless millions around the globe. It does many things its own way, and a lot of them seem admirable: When it went public, for example, it insisted on a process that would circumvent Wall Street's usual insider cronyism and make Google stock equally available to anyone who could afford five shares.

But when you're suddenly richer than John D. Rockefeller and operating on a scale that invites Microsoft comparisons, can a backlash be far behind?

Both the APA's Adler and Kelly, the digital journalist, think it's already here. They cite, among other things, Google's morally questionable decision to abide by political restrictions placed on it by the Chinese government; the American public's dismay when it discovered just how much of its private online behavior gets filed away in Google computers; and the usual human reaction, as Kelly puts it, "to large success of every type."

Fair use or not, this might not be the ideal time for Google to claim the right to digitize every single book in the world.

The publishers' and authors' lawsuits are in the discovery phase, which likely will drag on for months. It's not clear when the court will hear the merits of the fair use argument; Adler's best guess is the spring or summer of 2007.

Unless the two sides end up negotiating after all.

And here's where the outcome of this legal battle and the future of the book may begin to merge.

Everyone involved agrees that search helps people discover books they want. Everyone also agrees that in an ideal world, once those books are found, there'd be a quick way for the finders to pay to access the actual text — all of it or just part of it, whatever they need.

Under Google's copy-everything-without-permission plan, easy access to anything but "snippets" is denied for most copyrighted books. But with the right deal in place, copyright holders would get paid and Google could make Book Search a *whole* lot more useful.

When you ask Google executives directly whether they plan to offer some kind of print-on-demand service — as Amazon.com, for instance, with publishers' permission, already does — they can get a bit coy. "We don't really speculate about the future," Smith says, just minutes after he's noted — in response to a more general question — that "one of the interesting technologies to keep an eye on is print on demand."

But that's the future. Right now, five days a week, the Googlers are still backing trucks up to that Stanford loading dock.

It's anybody's guess when they'll get to the shelf where call number E169 D3 resides.

Things to Think About

1. Do you agree with Google's interpretation of the "fair use" provisions of copyright law? Explain the opposing positions. Why is the creation and retention of the digital copies a major point of contention?

2. What are the benefits of digitization to the citizenry at large? Provide evidence. Why did Stanford's head librarian jump on the Google bandwagon?

3. Do you agree with Keller's assertion that Google's use of copyrighted work does not hurt the marketplace? Explain. How would you compare this with arguments from the Recording Industry Association of America?

4. Do you agree with Keller's opinion as to the goal of the lawsuits? Do you see an ethical dilemma in the trade association's expectations? The others label their version of robots.txt as price. Explain.

5. Even Google allies cite concerns about ethical decision-making in regard to Google's reluctance to negotiate. What recent developments deter from the core values Google has chosen? Explain. How do these concerns impact the digitization project?

Key Terms

1. Crawlers

2. Data mining

FORUM 3

Personal Security Responsibility

Article Overview

Young adults are particularly vulnerable to identity theft, but uninformed and complacent consumers at any age are at great risk. Are you one of them? Have you thought of placing a fraud alert on your credit report that will prompt creditors to contact you for authorization, before opening any new accounts? Who are the three major credit reporting agencies to contact? Did you know that you can call 1-800-5 OPTOUT and request that credit card companies stop sending preapproved credit card applications to your house? Did you know that you are entitled to one free credit report each year (www.freecreditreportservice.com)? The list goes on…

Article: *How To Keep Your Personal Information Safe*

By MARY BETH MARKLEIN
August 2, 2006
USAToday.com

No one knows for sure how many college students have been victims of identity theft, but they are popular targets. Federal Trade Commission data show that 18- to 24-year-olds are the second highest risk group, after ages 25 to 34.

Students are attractive candidates in part because they are typically transient and have less credit history than more established adults.

That makes it more difficult to distinguish between a legitimate credit application and a fraudulent one, says Mike Cook of ID Analytics, a San Diego identity risk management company.

"If you are going to steal an identity, a student identity is a very good one to steal," he says.

Also, college students create risks for themselves. The popularity of social networking sites such as Facebook and Myspace has led to concerns that students disclose too much information about themselves without taking stock of the potential dangers of such activity.

A number of organizations, from the Federal Trade Commission to individual colleges, are developing campaigns aimed at helping consumers protect themselves.

Linda Foley of the San Diego based Identity Theft Resource Center offers these tips for students:

- Keep personal information in a locked box so even your roommate can't get it.

- Add a shredder to your list of back-to-school needs.

- Don't use your Social Security number for any reason other than tax and employment, to get a line of credit or for student load applications. If your school uses your Social Security number as an identified—whether it's on your student ID or a professor posting grades by Social Security number—lobby to change the policy.

- Don't be tempted by free T-shirts or other incentives to apply for credit cards at a table set up on campus.

- Know what the scams are, and don't respond to them. (One popular online scam called "phishing" involves a thief posing as a legitimate business asking you to provide sensitive data so they can "update their files" or "protect your data.")

This month, Foley's group will unveil a teen information program on its website. It will be available at www.idtheftcenter.org.

Things to Think About

1. Why is the college-age student among the two highest risk groups for identity theft? Examine Facebook and Myspace. Can you locate information that would be considered risky behavior? Describe.

2. Have you noticed a change in policy at your academic institution in regard to Social Security numbers? Explain. How can you help ensure that an identity thief cannot obtain credit in your name, even with your Social Security number and identification in hand?

3. What specific advice would you give others to avoid being victimized by phishing?

4. The article suggests that readers avoid completing unnecessary credit card applications, even to acquire free gifts as part of a marketing promotion. Can you think of other negative consequences that will result from this activity?

5. Research the recent highly publicized personal security breaches at Hewlett-Packard. What device does the author suggest should be part of a back-to-college shopping list in order to avoid pretexting? As Verizon files suit against Hewlett-Packard, what other suggestions are given to telephone customers? How could acceptance of the email with tracing software have been avoided?

Key Terms

1. Phishing

2. Pretexting

FORUM 4

Electronic Intrusions

Article Overview

Avicious cycle exists in cyberspace. Vulnerability researchers locate security holes; hackers use this research to develop malicious code and then post it on the Internet; cybercriminals use the malicious code to control the processors of vulnerable computers for criminal activity. With the number of malicious threats inflating 200% in just two years, what measures should be in place to protect consumers?

Article: *Cybercrooks constantly find new ways into PCs*

By BYRON ACOHIDO
August 2, 2006 10:14 PM ET
USA TODAY

LAS VEGAS — Apple loyalists take heed: Hackers and cyberthieves have begun targeting your beloved software.

Hacking security holes in Apple (AAPL) programs is in an early phase. And Apple owners have yet to experience the full brunt of cyberintrusions all too familiar to Microsoft (MSFT) customers.

But it's coming.

As 3,000 hackers and security experts convene here for the Black Hat cybersecurity convention this week, computer users at home and at work have more reason than ever to worry about an intruder sneaking onto their hard drives.

Sure, there hasn't been a headline-grabbing computer infection since the Zotob worm last August, and Zotob was a mere shadow of the dozens of worms that preceded it, such as Sasser, Blaster and Code Red.

What's happened is that cybercrime, like an antibiotic-resistant malady, has begun to mutate. The profit motive for cyberthieves to break into computers to steal identity data or use processing power to carry out fraud schemes has never been greater. Meanwhile, Microsoft has relentlessly shored up Windows, the operating system running on 90% of desktop PCs. Windows is no longer a fertile petri dish for fast-spreading infections.

In 2004, hackers — programmers, often self-taught, who relish testing the limits of computer code — blanketed the Internet with more than 30 globe-galloping Windows worms, self-spreading programs created to scour the Internet for computers to infiltrate. Today, with Windows more secure, hackers are flushing out vulnerabilities in popular software applications. Cyberthieves follow in their wake, gravitating to weak points in any program that's widely used — Web browsers, media players, spreadsheets — targeting individuals and small groups of users.

The most popular new routes: Microsoft's ubiquitous Internet Explorer Web browser and Office suite of programs, because they're the most widely deployed programs.

But vulnerability researchers — a global community of good-guy and bad-guy hackers — are also increasingly cracking popular applications such as Apple's iChat instant-messaging service, Mozilla's Firefox Web browser, Adobe's (ADBE) Flash website-authoring tool, even the MySpace social networking website.

"It's more than a Microsoft world," says Marc Maiffret, lead researcher at security firm eEye.

"People are starting to realize it's a lot easier to find vulnerabilities in third-party software that doesn't have the level of scrutiny of Microsoft products," he says.

While software vendors agree that security holes, once discovered, ought to be patched quickly, they've yet to adopt a common minimum standard for notifying customers and issuing a security patch, a small piece of software that fixes the problem.

To get a sense of where intrusions can happen, USA TODAY and tech security firm Secure Elements reviewed patches reported by Microsoft, Apple, Mozilla and Adobe to the Common Vulnerabilities and Exposures (CVE) list, overseen as a public service by tech management firm Mitre.

The list provides common names for publicly known security holes and is a rough indicator of which applications are attracting hackers' attention. "The CVE identifier is the most oranges-to-oranges comparison you can make," says Scott Carpenter, Secure Elements security director.

Each of the four companies also responded to a USA TODAY questionnaire about patching policies. The analysis found that since January 2005, Apple has had to fix 67% more security holes than Microsoft. Apple issued security patches for 262 vulnerabilities, compared with 157 for Microsoft, 150 for Mozilla and 46 for Adobe.

In the tiered world of hacking specialists, researchers take the lead in discovering and disclosing new vulnerabilities. Someone else usually creates and publishes malicious programs that take advantage of the flaw, simply to prove it can be done. And, finally, a crook, intent on breaching vulnerable computers, actually puts the malicious code into action.

Such malicious programs, known as "proof-of-concept exploits," have been published for at least 10 recently discovered Apple vulnerabilities. Once such code is posted on the Internet, "It's like having a loaded gun sitting there," says Rohit Dhamankar, lead security architect for 3Com's TippingPoint. If there's a way to profit, crooks don't hesitate to put a published malicious program to work.

Security experts say it's very likely that numerous Apple attacks are circulating undetected on the Internet, given that cybercrooks are more clever than ever about covering their tracks.

At least two Apple attacks have been detected this year: a worm spreading through a flaw in Apple's iChat instant-messaging service and a malicious program distributed via its Safari browser that turns control of the Mac over to the intruder.

Apple, which has been running TV and Web ads touting its immunity to security problems, contends that any threat to its customers is negligible, because the number of known Apple security breaches is minuscule.

"There has never been a widespread attack on any software Apple has produced," says Apple spokeswoman Lynn Fox. "We take security very seriously."

Yet hackers and intruders have taken heed that 25 million Apple Mac users and 58 million iPod owners might be worth some attention. Six of the Apple security patches issued this year have been for vulnerabilities identified in the Mac Safari browser; 16 for QuickTime, the media player supporting iPods.

"People are starting to realize Mac adoption is on the rise, so they're spending more time exploiting Mac systems and Mac software," says Alfred Huger, senior director of engineering at computer-security giant Symantec.

IPod owners who use iTunes and QuickTime media players on Windows PCs may be particularly ripe for attack, says security researcher Maiffret. That's because Apple prompts Windows users to voluntarily install upgraded versions of the programs but does not alert them when such feature upgrades include important security fixes.

The user "might potentially skip it because he doesn't necessarily care about a new version just then," says Maiffret.

Favorite routes

It's true that hackers and cybercrooks continue to spend most of their time devising attempts to breach about 820 million Windows PCs in use worldwide. Security firm McAfee says the number of malicious threats recently surpassed 200,000, ballooning 200% in two years, most of it aimed at Microsoft. Favorite new attack routes include Microsoft Office and Internet Explorer; hackers find fresh vulnerabilities and write attack code, then thieves begin breaching PCs, often before Microsoft can make a patch available.

Recent Office attacks have taken the form of e-mail directed to workers within targeted companies. Often arriving on a Monday, when in-boxes are overflowing, and appearing to come from a trusted source, the messages entice the victim to click on an infected Word, PowerPoint or Excel attachment. Opening or saving it turns control of the PC over to the intruder, who can then steal sensitive data and probe deeper into the company's internal network.

Internet Explorer attacks lurk in an array of forms on tainted Web pages. Usually all a victim has to do is click on a link to go to the tainted page where the breach takes place.

To make the point that Web browsers have almost unlimited security holes, researcher HD Moore, co-founder of Metasploit, a security advocacy group, published one new browser vulnerability each day for the month of July. Most were for Internet Explorer, but some exposed flaws in Firefox, Opera and Safari.

Moore, a renowned hacker and featured speaker at the Black Hat conference, says he intended to "illuminate the different classes of bugs and give examples of how they can be triggered." He says he wants to equip companies to shore up security of their browsers.

In its 10th year, Black Hat has attracted a record number of attendees. Network technicians swarm the meeting rooms at Caesars Palace to hear tips from hackers and security experts on how to defend their companies from mushrooming attacks.

"The bad guys are really stepping up their game," says Jeremiah Grossman, founder and chief technology officer of WhiteHat Security. "No more fun and games. The attacks are much more malicious and profit-driven."

Lessons learned

Despite Office and Internet Explorer emerging as prime targets du jour, Microsoft has won praise for reversing its historical nonchalance about security. It's taken four years. Chairman Bill Gates in January 2002 suddenly shut down all work on Windows and dispatched all of his Windows software engineers to security boot camp.

Windows had come under withering assault by virus writers probing the many open features that made it child's play to remotely access and control Windows PCs inside corporate networks. At the time, the company had only a handful of security specialists. Today, it has more than 650 full-time security positions.

At the convention Thursday, Microsoft finds itself in the position of showing off cutting-edge security features in Windows Vista, due out early next year, and coaching others on how to go about developing secure software.

"We've learned some lessons, sometimes painfully, and we want to share that with the industry so all software products from all vendors can be safer," says Stephen Toulouse, Microsoft's security program manager.

Apple does not have a corporate presence at Black Hat. One measure of the gap in security readiness between the two tech giants: Microsoft issues patches on a regular schedule and assigns a rating to each vulnerability; Apple issues patches periodically and does not use a rating system.

"Nobody does anything about security until you absolutely have to," says Richard Stiennon, chief analyst at security research firm IT-Harvest. "Once Apple faces the repercussions of a massive exploit, then they will change their behavior."

Things to Think About

1. How can cyberthieves profit from using your processing power?

2. Why is the Windows operating system less vulnerable to security holes than Internet Explorer and Office, Apple ichat and Mozilla, and third-party software? Research the Common Vulnerabilities and Exposures (CVE) list provided by Mitre. How is this site helpful to the end user?

3. Why is Apple's list of vulnerabilities most surprising? Why are hackers more focused on exploiting Mac systems and Mac software? Does Apple have a responsibility to its customers to notify them of important security fixes in upgraded versions of the software? How could Apple learn from Microsoft's lead? Do you agree with Stiennon's assertion as to the reason Apple has not followed suit?

4. What kind of minimum standard notification would you suggest for notifying customers and issuing a security patch? Have you experienced notification issues at your school or business? When and how are users most vulnerable? Be specific.

5. What is the legal argument for allowing malicious code to be published, when it is known that "proof-of-concept exploits" will be used to breach vulnerable computers? Is it ethical to publish malicious code? Are there any instances of when publishing malicious code is productive?

Key Terms

1. Proof-of-concept exploits

2. CVE list

FORUM 5

Security in the Information Economy

Article Overview

Some of us still recall the "Chernobyl" virus along with the deep sense of frustration and violation that accompanied it. Never had we imagined six years ago that having our hard drives deleted might be considered a minor hassle compared to the concerns of virus attacks today. Just when most users have mastered back-up procedures, especially in consideration of post 9/11 lessons learned, virus writers now consider the hard drive a very important host to keep intact. For those with malicious intent, the hard drive is useful for a variety of purposes, such as to store software. Hackers do not break into computer systems just for access to stored information anymore.

Article: *Why Break In? The Reasons Vary*

August 2, 2006
USA TODAY

A USA TODAY review of 109 computer-related security breaches reported by 76 college campuses since January 2005 found that about 70% involved hacking — breaking into or gaining unauthorized access to a computer system.

But while campus data breaches, whether hacking or not, may have compromised personal information of more than 2.8 million people, identity theft was not necessarily a motive.

In some cases, the motivation appeared to be narrow in scope. Prosecutors said last week, for example, that two former California State University-Northridge students illegally accessed a professor's computer network to change grades.

In April, a former computer engineering student at the University of Delaware was put on probation and fined $10,000 after he sent an e-mail through a professor's account telling students an exam date had been changed.

And last year, more than 100 applicants to Harvard Business School were able to get an early look at whether they had been accepted, thanks to a hacker.

In other cases, hackers were traced to overseas locations. At George Mason University in Fairfax, Va., last year, the culprit turned out to be a teenager in the Netherlands who was looking to store music.

In a pair of incidents reported last July at the University of Colorado at Boulder and traced to France and Eastern Europe, officials said the hackers appeared to be downloading or storing movies. Ohio University officials suspect a similar motive behind a string of breaches there.

USA TODAY examined data compiled by the Privacy Rights Clearinghouse and the Identity Theft Resource Center, both of them non-profit groups based in San Diego. It also did its own search of publicly documented incidents.

Breaches that primarily involved patients at university hospitals and medical centers were excluded. Student health centers, bookstores and similar venues were included. Also excluded were breaches that did not involve computers. For example, a passerby found a bag containing paper documents with names, Social Security numbers and other data on an estimated 834 students at Anderson (S.C.) College in a parking lot off campus.

Other reasons for breaches:

- 12% (13 incidents) involved exposure online, often inadvertent. Officials at Montclair (N.J.) State University discovered last year that names and Social Security numbers of 9,100 undergraduates had been posted on the Internet for nearly four months after a student found a link to a school website that listed his name, major and Social Security number.

- 15% (16) involved the theft of a laptop or other hardware.

- 4% (four) had other causes. Officials at Stark State College of Technology in Jackson Township, Ohio, for example, attributed an incident reported last year to a software glitch.

Things to Think About

1. Is the punishment of a $10,000 fine excessive for the University of Delaware student? Explain.

2. It may appear that all 9,100 students victimized by the Montclair State University incident failed to protect themselves by following a simple measure of personal security maintenance. Explain.

3. How can the practice of examining data compiled by such non-profit organizations as the Privacy Rights Clearinghouse assist organizations in maintaining security?

4. Assuming the data stored was harmless and that there were no risks of personal data retrieval, what other damages are created by the incidents at George Mason and University of Colorado for the victims?

5. What concerns are raised in relation to the type of software stored by the hackers in the George Mason and University of Colorado incidents?

Key Terms

1. Privacy Rights Clearinghouse

2. Identity Theft Resource Center

FORUM 6

Electronic Social Responsibility

Article Overview

“What will the neighbors think?,” she chided. My grandmother strongly disapproved of anyone who acted in a way that was known to attract, what she considered, “undue” attention. When she observed a person deemed of this sort, she labeled the individual an “exhibitionist”. Familiar clichés were, “don’t wear your feelings on your shirtsleeves”, “don’t air your dirty laundry”, and “good fences make good neighbors.” Privacy and reputation represented important social values. With the advent of social networking, is it possible that our values have shifted? Or is social networking merely another example of consumer exploitation by lucrative business ventures? Do all those participating truly understand both the short term and long term consequences of their actions? Are they aware that “what is said on the Internet may stay on the Internet?”

Article: *A Web of Exhibitionists*

By ROBERT J. SAMUELSON
September 20, 2006
WashingtonPost.com; p. A25

Call it the ExhibitioNet. It turns out that the Internet has unleashed the greatest outburst of mass exhibitionism in human history. Everyone may not be entitled, as Andy Warhol once suggested, to 15 minutes of fame. But everyone is entitled to strive for 15 minutes — or 30, 90 or much more. We have blogs, “social networking” sites (MySpace.com, Facebook), YouTube and all their rivals. Everything about these sites is a scream for attention. Look at me. Listen to me. Laugh with me — or at me.

This is no longer fringe behavior. MySpace has 56 million American “members.” Facebook — which started as a site for college students and has expanded to high school students and others — has 9 million members. (For the unsavvy: MySpace and Facebook allow members to post personal pages with pictures and text.) About 12 million American adults (8 percent of Internet users) blog, estimates the Pew Internet & American Life Project. YouTube — a site where anyone can post home videos — says 100 million videos are watched daily.

Exhibitionism is now a big business. In 2005 Rupert Murdoch’s News Corp. bought MySpace for a reported $580 million. All these sites aim to make money, mainly through ads and fees. What’s interesting culturally and politically is that their popularity contradicts the belief that people fear the Internet will violate their right to privacy. In reality, millions of Americans are gleefully discarding — or at least cheerfully compromising — their right to privacy. They're posting personal and intimate stuff in places where thousands or millions can see it.

People seem to crave popularity or celebrity more than they fear the loss of privacy. Some of this extroversion is crass self-promotion. The Internet is a cheap way to advertise ideas and projects. Anyone can post a video on YouTube, free; you can start a blog free (some companies don't charge for "hosting" a site). Last week a popular series of videos — Lonelygirl15 — on YouTube was revealed to be a scripted drama, written by three aspiring filmmakers, and not a teenager's random meditations.

But the ExhibitioNet is more than a marketing tool. The same impulse that inspires people to spill their guts on "Jerry Springer" or to participate in "reality TV" shows (MTV's "The Real World" and its kin) has now found a mass outlet. MySpace aims at an 18-to-34-year-old audience; many of the pages are proudly raunchy. U.S. News & World Report recently described MySpace as "Lake Wobegon gone horribly wrong: a place where all the women are fast [and] the men are hard-drinking."

The blogosphere is often seen as mainly a political arena. That's a myth. According to the Pew estimates, most bloggers (37 percent) focus on "my life and personal experiences." Politics and government are a very distant second (11 percent), followed by entertainment (7 percent) and sports (6 percent). Even these figures may exaggerate the importance of politics. Half of bloggers say they're mainly interested in expressing themselves "creatively."

Self-revelation and attitude are what seem to appeal. Heather Armstrong maintains one of the most popular personal blogs (Dooce.com). "I never had a cup of coffee until I was 23-years-old," she writes. "I had premarital sex for the first time at age 22, but BY GOD I waited an extra year for the coffee." She started her blog in 2001, got fired from her job as a Web designer in Los Angeles for writing about work ("My advice to you is BE YE NOT SO STUPID."), became "an unemployed drunk," got married and moved to Salt Lake City, where she had a child.

Armstrong is a graceful and often funny writer. ("I am no longer a practicing Mormon or someone who believes that Rush Limbaugh speaks to God. My family is understandably disappointed.") The popular site now has so many ads that her husband quit his job. Recent postings include an ode to her 2-year-old daughter, a story about her dog and a plug for her friend Maggie's book, "No One Cares What You Had for Lunch: 100 Ideas for Your Blog." Idea No. 32: breaking up. Naturally, Armstrong expounds on her busted relationships.

Up to a point, the blogs and "social networking" sites represent new forms of electronic schmoozing — extensions of e-mail and instant messaging. What's different is the undiluted passion for self-publicity. But even among the devoted, there are occasional doubts about whether this is all upside. Facebook recently announced a new service. Its computers would regularly scan the pages of its members and flash news of the latest postings as headlines to their friends' pages. There was an uproar. Suppose your girlfriend decides she's had enough. The potential headline to your pals: "Susan dumps George." Countless students regarded the relentless electronic snooping and automatic messaging as threatening — "stalking," as many put it. Facebook modified the service by allowing members to opt out.

The larger reality is that today's exhibitionism may last a lifetime. What goes on the Internet often stays on the Internet. Something that seems harmless, silly or merely impetuous today may seem offensive, stupid or reckless in two weeks, two years or two decades. Still, we are clearly at a special moment. Thoreau famously remarked that "the mass of men lead lives of quiet desperation." Thanks to technology, that's no longer necessary. People can now lead lives of noisy and ostentatious desperation. Or at least they can try.

Things to Think About

1. The author suggests that part of the popularity of Internet exhibitionism is economics. Explain.

2. Describe the market for social hub sites. Why might young people be more inclined to "bare all" on the Internet? Does an understanding of "boundaries" come at a later age?

3. What can be learned from Heather Armstrong's success? Explain

4. Why did most Facebook customers regard the new service of "news flashing" as electronic snooping? What do their reactions suggest about their assumptions related to the exposure of their postings?

5. Explain the author's comment that "What goes on the Internet often stays on the Internet".

Key Terms

1. PEW Reports

2. Electronic stalking

FORUM 7

Information Asymmetry

Article Overview

Information has always been known to economists as a powerful force. In the past, experts have often used their informational advantage to serve their own agenda, rather than that of their customers. The advent of the Internet, however, has shifted the disproportionate balance of power to the consumer. The authors suggest that the strength of the power of information is determined by who is in control of it and how it is manipulated.

Article: *The Ku Klux Klan and Real-Estate Agents*

Excerpt from *Freakonomics*
By STEVEN D. LEVITT and STEPHEN J. DUBNER
Copyright © 2005
William Morrow, an imprint of Harper Collins Publishers

In the late 1990s, the price of term life insurance fell dramatically. This posed something of a mystery, for the decline had no obvious cause. Other types of insurance, including health and automobile and homeowners' coverage, were certainly not falling in price. Nor had there been any radical changes among insurance companies, insurance brokers, or the people who buy term life insurance. So what happened?

The Internet happened. In the spring of 1996, Quotesmith.com became the first of several websites that enabled a customer to compare, within seconds, the price of term insurance sold by dozens of different companies. For such websites, term life insurance was a perfect product. Unlike other forms of insurance—including whole life insurance, which is a far more complicated financial instrument—term life policies are fairly homogeneous: one thirty-year, guaranteed policy for $1 million is essentially identical to the next. So what really matters is the price. Shopping around for the cheapest policy, a process that had been convoluted and time-consuming, was suddenly made simple. With customers able to instantaneously find the cheapest policy, the more expensive companies had no choice but to lower their prices. Suddenly customers were paying $1 billion less a year for term life insurance.

It is worth noting that these websites only listed prices; they didn't even sell the policies. So it wasn't really insurance they were peddling. Like Stetson Kennedy, they were dealing in information. (Had the Internet been around when Kennedy infiltrated the Klan, he probably would have rushed home after each meeting and blogged his brains out.) To be sure, there are differences between exposing the Ku Klux Klan and exposing insurance companies' high premiums. The Klan trafficked in secret information whose secrecy engendered fear, while insurance prices were less a secret than a set of facts dispensed in a way that made comparisons difficult. But in both instances, the dissemination of the information diluted its power. As Supreme Court Justice Louis D. Brandeis once wrote, "Sunlight is said to be the best of disinfectants."

Information is a beacon, a cudgel, an olive branch, a deterrent, depending on who wields it and how. Information is so powerful that the *assumption* of information, even if information does not actually exist, can have a sobering effect. Consider the case of a one-day-old car.

The day that a car is driven off the lot is the worst day in its life. For it instantly loses as much as a quarter of its value. This might seem absurd, but we know it to be true. A new car that was bought for $20,000 cannot be resold for more than perhaps $15,000. Why? Because the only person who might logically want to resell a brand-new car is someone who found the car to be a lemon. So even if the car isn't a lemon, a potential buyer assumes that it is. He assumes that the seller has some information about the car that he, the buyer, does not have—and the seller is punished for this assumed information.

And if the car *is* a lemon? The seller would do well to wait a year to sell it. By then, the suspicion of lemonness will have faded; by then, some people will be selling their perfectly good year-old cars, and the lemon can blend in with them, likely selling for more than it is truly worth.

It is common for one party to a transaction to have better information than another party. In the parlance of economists, such a case is known as an information asymmetry. We accept as a verity of capitalism that someone (usually an expert) knows more than someone else (usually a consumer). But information asymmetries everywhere have in fact been mortally wounded by the Internet.

Information is the currency of the Internet. As a medium, the Internet is brilliantly efficient at shifting information from the hands of those who have it into the hands of those who do not. Often, as in the case of term life insurance prices, the information existed but in a woefully scattered way. (In such instances, the Internet acts like a gigantic horseshoe magnet waved over an endless sea of haystacks, plucking the needle out of each one.) Just as Stetson Kennedy accomplished what no journalist, do-gooder, or prosecutor could, the Internet has accomplished what no consumer advocate could: it has vastly shrunk the gap between the experts and the public.

The Internet has proven particularly fruitful for situations in which a face-to-face encounter with an expert might actually *exacerbate* the problem of asymmetrical information—situations in which an expert uses his informational advantage to make us feel stupid or rushed or cheap or ignoble. Consider a scenario in which your loved one has just died and now the funeral director—who knows that you know next to nothing about his business and are under emotional duress to boot—steers you to the $7,000 mahogany casket. Or consider the automobile dealership: the salesman does his best to obscure the car's base price under a mountain of add-ons and incentives. Later, however, in the cool-headed calm of your home, you can use the Internet to find out exactly how much the dealer paid the manufacturer for that car. Or you might just log on to www.TributeDirect.com and buy that mahogany casket yourself for just $3,200, delivered overnight. Unless you decide to spend $2,995 for "The Last Hole" (a casket with golf scenes) or "Memories of the Hunt" (featuring big-racked bucks and other prey) or one of the much cheaper models that the funeral director somehow failed even to mention.

Things to Think About

1. Why was term life insurance an easy product to report to customers engaged in comparative shopping? Before the availability of the Internet, would the information have been available for consumers to consider? Explain how the dissemination of this information diluted the power of some insurance companies to overcharge customers.

2. Explain how the assumption of information, even if the information does not really exist, can impact an organization. How does this relate to how a car may lose up to a quarter of its value when it is driven off the lot?

3. Is "sunlight the best of disinfectants"? How have information asymmetries "been mortally wounded" by the Internet?

4. With asymmetrical information balanced by the currency of the Internet, what marketing strategies may better serve the automobile dealer or funeral director? Does the availability of information help achieve more ethical business practices?

5. How did Stetson Kennedy expose the Ku Klux Klan? How did the dissemination of the information dilute its power?

Key Terms

1. Information asymmetry

2. Information

FORUM 8

Expanding Processing Power

Article Overview

Economic growth may be achieved when economies of scale are realized. When more data is manipulated on a larger scale, with borrowed power allowing for lower costs, economies of scale are achieved. Industry, government and education must responsibly seek to expand computing resources in a cost efficient manner, while enabling scientific research to advance the cure of debilitating diseases. Cyberthiefs beware! We may be donating our processing power to the World Community Grid with IBM providing for our security.

Article: *'Grids' extend schools' processing power*

September 20, 2006
eSchool News

Worldwide spending on grid computing is expected to top $24 billion in five years. Grid computing, in which computers are linked across a giant network like an electricity grid, has been used for years to scan radio signals from outer space for signs of extraterrestrial life, help mathematicians find the largest prime number, and so on. Now, an increasing number of colleges and universities, businesses, and even K-12 school systems are tapping into the power of grid computing to extend their computing resources.

As Habitat for Humanity and the Girl Scouts recruited students at Meredith College in North Carolina willing to volunteer their time, a team from IBM staked out the campus dining hall with a softer request, seeking only to borrow the calculating power of the students' idle computers.

"It's easy, which people like to hear," said Rebecca Thompson, a 20-year-old senior. "I'll be talking [to friends] and helping fight AIDS at the same time."

Thompson's college-issued laptop, when she's not using it for class, is part of the World Community Grid, an IBM-supported network that senses when private computers are sitting idle, then taps the machines to perform complicated calculations ordinarily performed on expensive supercomputers.

The grid is being used by researchers at the Cancer Institute of New Jersey in conjunction with teachers and students at Rutgers University to develop cures for cancer, AIDS, and other diseases—and by IBM to demonstrate the potential of borrowing power from the more than 650 million PCs estimated in use around the world.

Grid networks have been used for years to scan radio signals from outer space for signs of extraterrestrial life, to help mathematicians find the largest prime number, and to narrow down the number of potential smallpox vaccines to a few dozen. Now, an increasing number of colleges and universities, businesses, and even K-12 school systems are tapping into the power of grids to extend their computing resources.

Earlier this year, the Southeastern Universities Research Association (SURA), a group of 24 colleges and universities across 15 states, joined together to form a supercomputer grid that reportedly will give researchers the ability to perform up to 10 trillion calculations a second, paving the way for speedier advancements in the fields of science and medicine.

"The old model used to be that every researcher got his own computer," said Art Vandenberg, director of advanced campus services at Georgia State, one of the first universities to participate in the project, in an interview with the Associated Press in August. "But by partnering, we create a fabric we can all get to."

For Georgia State, the grid quadruples researchers' computing power, allowing scientists to run in a week computer simulations that once would have taken a month. The equipment for that grid, too, is being provided by IBM, which sold the processors, wires, and other pieces to each college at a deeply discounted rate. Georgia State paid $585,000 for a computer that would have cost more than $2 million, Vandenberg said.

"This is the internet equivalent of a 100-lane highway," said Greg Kubiak, director of relations and communications for SURA (see story: http://www.eschoolnews.com/news/showStory.cfm?ArticleID=6506).

Other leading research universities, including Carnegie Mellon and Purdue, have launched similar projects.

And interest in the field appears to be growing. Even video-game manufacturers are getting into the act. According to a Sept. 18 report on the news web site CNN.com, when Sony Corp. releases its long-awaited PlayStation 3 video game console in November, users will have the option of donating the technology that powers these advanced gaming machines to ongoing research efforts conducted via the internet.

Working with researchers at Stanford University's Folding@home project, Sony engineers have developed a software program that PlayStation 3 users can download to give researchers access to the console's processor when the machine is not in use, as long as the power is switched on, they say.

Engineers say the game system's high-powered Cell Broadband Engine, which it uses to run realistic video games, might play a central role in helping researchers find cures to debilitating diseases, including Parkinson's, Alzheimer's, and amyotrophic lateral sclerosis, better known as Lou Gherig's disease. A version of the same chip used to power the PlayStation 3 game console also reportedly is being used by IBM to run a new supercomputer for the Department of Energy. According to CNN, that machine is capable of processing up to 1 trillion calculations per second.

Last week, leading practitioners met in Washington, D.C., as part of a national conference called GridWorld to discuss developments and prospects in grid computing.

Despite the enthusiasm of researchers, the concept has its problems. For one, "there's still an awful lot of complexity and confusion on how to put these things together," said William Fellows, who runs grid research studies at The 451 Group, an independent technology industry analyst company.

The technology got its name because, like the electricity grid, users can access power far away rather than having a power plant of their own, said Ian Foster, a computer science professor at the University of Chicago and Argonne National Laboratory who is credited as one of the technology's founders.

Complicated scientific problems are divided into small pieces and distributed to individual computers on the grid. The small pieces of data are processed simultaneously, cutting research time by months or years. The results are delivered back to a central computer, where the results are assembled into an answer.

Since 1999, nearly 5.5 million internet users have signed up to run SETI@Home, which combs through celestial radio signals for patterns that might be communication from another world.

The Grid.org cancer research project electronically tested 3.5 billion molecules against 12 cancer-causing proteins in three years. It found millions of potential drug candidates, hundreds of which were tested in labs. About 2 percent showed cancer-fighting potential, far more candidates than other methods have generated.

As grid computing's promise of cheaper, more flexible processing power has caught on in science, business has taken notice. Insight Research Corp., a New Jersey-based telecommunications market research company, estimates worldwide spending on grid computing will grow from $1.8 billion this year to about $24.5 billion in 2011.

Most of the top 20 banks in the U.S. and Europe already use some kind of grid computing, often to run statistical models that predict risk or shape asset portfolios, Fellows said. Not only is grid computing cheaper than buying supercomputers; the practice also hints at the ability to outsource advanced computer analysis, such as analytical efforts aimed at forecasting future events.

IBM already has about 500 commercial customers for its grid computing services, including scientific research centers and businesses in aerospace, pharmaceuticals, and financial services, said Ken King, IBM's vice president of grid computing. The company also is linking China's higher-education institutions to allow better research collaboration, he said.

Christopher Willard, an analyst at research firm IDC, said providers such as IBM will profit by allowing clients to avoid buying more computers than they use regularly and accommodate emergency needs for computing power, as well as by serving medium-sized businesses and schools that don't have the money for costly computer systems.

Participation in IBM's World Community Grid, the network that Meredith College students are part of, is open to companies, associations, universities, and individuals.

For people looking to donate their computing power to these and other research efforts, administrators say the only costs associated with the project are a potential increase in participants' electric bills, because their computers will be constantly processing information, not sitting idle, and—because the connection is web-based—a small spike in monthly payments to local internet service providers, though this depends on existing agreements.

In terms of computing power, each project operated by the grid—whether for cancer research, AIDS research, and so on—reportedly has its own requirements, and users are asked to choose a particular project when signing up. According to the World Community Grid web site, there are at least 410,000 participants.

"I know when I take a shower or go down the hall, I could be using the time that [my computer is] on and devote it to the project," said Whitney Rains, 19, a Meredith College sophomore. "A lot of good could be contributed if everyone does a little bit."

The challenges to widespread use of grid computing are not all technical. Foster, the technology's pioneer, said by its very nature, grid computing involves letting go of control over who gets to see data and who has access to machines people think of as their own.

"What we're about is resource sharing for purposes of collaboration and increased flexibility. That has to be accompanied by the necessary sociological changes as well," Foster said.

Reaching out to people who don't make computing their profession—as IBM is doing with the World Computing Grid—also brings up questions about security, Foster said. There are questions about whether being linked to a worldwide network might leave a computer vulnerable to viruses, or expose a user's personal data.

But IBM's King said data flowing in and out of its servers are continuously monitored and bad things blocked—and the students at Meredith College don't seem worried.

"There's so many other ways [hackers] can get in," Thompson said. "But if I'm going down, IBM is going down. I trust them and trust their technology."

Things to Think About

1. How is grid computing like an electricity grid? How are video-game manufacturers and video-game users contributing?

2. How is the World Community Grid focused on demonstrating the potential of borrowing power from the more than 650 million PCs estimated in use in the world? Why is there a potential increase in participants' electric bills? What other expenses may be incurred? Would this deter your participation? What is the status of participation now?

3. How is grid computing used in business and government? Could large global grids have political implications?

4. What technical challenges exist to widespread use of grid computing? What sociological and security challenges exist? Do you agree with Thompson's rationale for trusting IBM to keep her data secure? Explain.

5. How does grid computing differ from the old model of extending resources? What is the potential for outsourcing?

Key Terms

1. Cell broadband engine

2. Supercomputer

FORUM 9

Technology Addiction

Article Overview

Her 21-year-old son, Sean, was found dead in front of his computer, with the video game visible on his computer screen. In his memory, Liz Woolley founded Online Gamers Anonymous in 2002. By adopting the Alcoholics Anonymous 12 step addiction recovery model to help gamers recover, she hopes to help tens of thousands of self-proclaimed addicted gamers to quit — but not before she takes on the video gaming industry. Will Liz Woolley have your support?

Article: *Lost in an Online Fantasy World*

By OLGA KHAZAN
August 18, 2006 3:52 PM
WashingtonPost.com

As Virtual Universes Grow, So Do Ranks of the Game-Obsessed

They are war heroes, leading legions into battle through intricately designed realms. They can be sorcerers or space pilots, their identities woven into a world so captivating, it is too incredible to ever leave. Unfortunately, some of them don't.

Video games have often been portrayed as violence-ridden vehicles for teen angst. But after 10 people in South Korea — mostly teenagers and young adults — died last year from game-addiction causes, including one man who collapsed in an Internet cafe after playing an online game for 50 hours with few breaks, some began to see a new technological threat.

Participation in massively multiplayer online role-playing games, also called MMORPGs or MMOs, has skyrocketed from less than a million subscribers in the late 1990s to more than 13 million worldwide in 2006. With each new game boasting even more spectacular and immersive adventures, new ranks of gamers are drawn to their riveting story lines. Like gambling, pornography or any other psychological stimulant, these games have the potential to thrill, engross and completely overwhelm.

The most widely played MMO, Blizzard Entertainment's World of Warcraft, has 6.5 million players worldwide, most of whom play 20 to 22 hours per week. Thousands can be logged in simultaneously to four different WoW servers (each its own self-contained "realm"), interacting with players across the globe in a vast virtual fantasy setting full of pitched battles and other violent adventures.

Brady Mapes, a 24-year-old computer programmer from Gaithersburg, Md., and an avid WoW fan, calls it a "highly addictive game — it sucks the life out of you."

An MMO differs from an offline game in that the game world evolves constantly as each players' actions directly or indirectly influence the lives of other players' characters. In WoW, players can simply attack one another, interact with the environment, or role-play in more complex relationships. More time playing means greater virtual wealth and status, as well as access to higher game levels and more-exciting content.

In addition, online gamers can join teams or groups (called "guilds" in WoW) that tackle game challenges cooperatively. Fellow team members see membership as a commitment and expect participation in virtual raids and other joint activities. The constant interaction with other players can lead to friendships and personal connections.

'All I Could Think About Was Playing'

"The main reason people are playing is because there are other people out there," said Dmitri Williams, an assistant professor at the University of Illinois at Urbana-Champaign, who has researched the social impacts of MMOs. "People know your name, they share your interests, they miss you when you leave."

As MMO fan sites filled with raving gamers proliferate, so have online-addiction help blogs, where desperate recluses and gamers' neglected spouses search for a way out.

"I don't want to do everything with [my husband], but it would be nice to have a meaningful conversation once in awhile," writes one pregnant wife on Everquest Daily Grind, a blog for those affected by excessive use of another popular fantasy MMO. "He does not have much interest in the baby so far, and I am worried that after it is born, he will remain the same while I am struggling to work and take care of the baby."

Another gamer writes that she was angry at her boyfriend for introducing her to online gaming, which began consuming her life at the expense of her personal and academic well-being.

"But I think deleting [your] character doesn't work, because the game haunts you," she said. "All I could think about was playing."

Kimberly Young, who has treated porn and chat-room addicts since 1994 at her Center for Internet Addiction Recovery, said that in the past year video game fixation has grown more than anything else.

"In MMOs, people lead wars and receive a lot of recognition," Young said. "It's hard to stop and go clean your room. Real life is much less interesting."

The trend echoes across the continents, with game-addiction treatment centers cropping up in China in 2005 and this summer in Amsterdam. In South Korea, where 70 percent of the population has broadband Internet access, the Korea Agency for Digital Opportunity offers government-funded counseling for the game-hooked.

'The Real World Gets Worse'

The games are set up to be lengthy, with a quest taking six hours or more to complete. The organization of players into cooperative teams creates a middle-school-esque atmosphere of constant peer pressure.

"You're letting other people down if you quit," Young said. "If you are good, the respect becomes directly reinforcing."

According to research performed by Nick Yee, a Stanford graduate student and creator of the Daedalus Project, an online survey of more than 40,000 MMO players, the average player is 26 years old; most hold full-time jobs. Seventy percent have played for 10 hours straight at some point, and about 45 percent would describe themselves as "addicted."

Yee believes escapism to be the best predictor of excessive gaming. A person who plays MMOs in order to avoid real-life problems, rather than simply for entertainment or socialization, is more likely to experience what he calls "problematic usage."

"People feel like they lack control in real life, and the game gives them a social status and value that they are less and less able to achieve in the real world," Yee said. "As a result, the real world gets worse and the virtual world gets better in comparison."

Liz Woolley, a Wisconsin software analyst and veteran of Alcoholics Anonymous, founded Online Gamers Anonymous in May 2002 by adapting AA's 12-step addiction recovery model to help gamers quit cold-turkey. Woolley recommends getting professional help for underlying issues and finding other hobbies and real-world activities to replace gaming.

"Addicts want to live in a fantasy life because you can't do a 'do-over' in real life," she said. "It can be hard to accept. You have to let them know, 'Hey, this is real life. Learn to deal with it.'"

'Every Player Has a Choice'

"People are reluctant to point a finger at themselves," said Jason Della Rocca, executive director of the International Game Developers Association. Excessive use "is a reflection of friction in that person's life. They shouldn't use the game as a scapegoat."

Casual gamers may find it difficult to advance to the game's highest levels in the face of more dedicated rivals, such as Mapes, the Gaithersburg WoW fan, whose highest-level warrior character is a force to be reckoned with. "If I go up against someone who only plays for one to two hours, I'll decimate them," he said. "There are other games out there if you only want to play a couple hours at a time."

That dedication sometimes pushes Mapes to see the game as more of a chore than a pastime. "Sometimes I realize that I'm not having any fun, but I just can't stop," he said.

Several of the MMO researchers interviewed for this story pointed out that many game companies employ psychologists who analyze the games and suggest ways to make them easier to play over long stretches of time.

Della Rocca argues that because online games' monthly subscription rates remain constant regardless of how many hours a subscriber spends on the network, developers profit less when gamers play more intensively.

The psychologists "monitor subjects playing the games in order to eliminate flaws and points of frustration," Della Rocca said. "The notion that we are trying to seduce gamers is a fabrication of people who don't understand how games are developed."

Since Blizzard Entertainment released WoW in 2004, calls to Online Gamers Anonymous have more than tripled, according to Woolley, who said the industry is directly at fault for the suffering of the people she tries to help.

"I think the game companies are nothing more than drug pushers," she said. "If I was a parent, I wouldn't let them in my house. It's like dropping your kids off at a bar and leaving them there."

The signs of excessive MMO use are similar to those of alcoholism or any other dependency — tolerance, withdrawal, lying or covering up, to name a few. However, many in the industry are hesitant to call it an addiction because, in the case of MMOs, the nature of the problem is based on how it affects the user's life, not the amount of time spent playing.

According to tvturnoff.org, Americans spend an average of 28 hours a week watching television, a fact that has yet to spawn a bevy of dependence clinics.

"If a person was reading novels excessively, we'd be less likely to call that 'addiction' because we value reading as culture," said the University of Illinois's Williams. "We see game play as frivolous due to our Protestant work ethic. There's plenty of anecdotal evidence out there to suggest this is a problem, but it's not the role of science to guess or bet."

Mapes, who has played other engrossing titles such as Medal of Honor and Diablo and eventually set them aside, said the decision to control excessive gaming is one any player can make.

"Ultimately, every player has a choice to stop," he said. "I've stopped before, and I've seen other people stop if they get burned out."

'No One Was Talking About It'

Woolley disagrees, especially after witnessing the bitter outcome of her son's Everquest obsession.

Shawn had played online games before, so she didn't suspect anything different when he picked up the newest MMO from Sony. Within months, Woolley said, Shawn withdrew from society, losing his job and apartment and moving back home to live a virtual life he found more fulfilling.

After a number of game-induced grand mal seizures sent Shawn, who was epileptic, to the emergency room repeatedly, he chose to pay ambulance bills rather than stop playing. The medical professionals he saw treated his external symptoms but dismissed his gaming condition.

"They told me, 'Be glad he's not addicted to something worse, like drugs,' and sent him home," Woolley said.

On Thanksgiving Day 2001, Woolley found 21-year-old Shawn dead in front of his computer after having committed suicide. Everquest was on the screen.

Readers' responses to an article written about the incident in a local Wisconsin paper poured in, and the national attention Shawn's story subsequently received prompted Woolley to start up a self-help Web site. In the four years since its launch, Online Gamers Anonymous (http://www.olganon.org/) has had 125 million hits and registered more than 2,000 members, Woolley said.

"I realized that gaming addiction was an underground epidemic affecting thousands of people, but no one was talking about it," she said. "I wasn't worried about pressure from the gaming industry. I thought, 'You already took my kid, you can't take anything else.'"

Things to Think About

1. Do you believe that fantasy game addiction can be compared to drug or alchohol addiction? Explain.

2. Gaming and simulation have long been recognized as effective in business, government and education. Why do you think computer fantasy games are different?

3. What evidence exists that this is a worldwide problem? What indication is there that the problem is recently worsening?

4. Do you believe it is ethical for the game manufacturers to hire psychologists to assist in the development of an addictive game? Do you believe Della Rocca's position? Explain.

5. What is the profile of the user? What social implications does Williams's research suggest?

Key Terms

1. MMOs

2. Center for Internet Addiction Recovery

FORUM 10

Application Software

Article Overview

The National Education Computing Conference in San Diego, in July of 2006, listed open source software as one of the emerging technologies necessary to build a technology infrastructure for effective teaching and learning communities. A few weeks before the conference, Bill Gates was featured in the media for his announcement to prepare for retirement from Microsoft in 2007 to focus on philanthropic endeavors. The scuttlebutt was that Bill is a genius; he is departing Microsoft at a time when Open Source Office software is gaining momentum. Do all educational institutions have a fiscal responsibility to seriously consider adoption of open source software?

Article: *More To Life Than The Office*

By STEVE HAM
July 3, 2006
Business Week Online

It's being updated furiously, but Microsoft's once-irreplaceable program now has some viable rivals

Don't expect Vijay Sonty to get any Customer of the Year awards from Microsoft Corp. The chief information officer for Florida's Broward County school system negotiated to pay only $14 per copy this year to outfit 40,000 employees with the Microsoft Office productivity suite. At retail, the bundle of the Word, Excel, Outlook, and PowerPoint lists at $399. But for Sonty, even a $14 annual subscription is still too expensive. That's why over the next three years he plans on cutting his Office purchases to 5,000. In its place, he's buying IBM Workplace, which not only includes Office-like applications for employees but also delivers online learning to the district's 274,000 students. His price: $4 per person per year.

For the vast majority of PC users, there's only one way to produce digital words and numbers—with Microsoft's Office. The ubiquitous suite of software programs has a 95% market share and 400 million copies in use. But now, for the first time in years, Microsoft faces some real competition. With a new version of Office set for release late this year, customers may take the opportunity to consider software that's less expensive and easier to use. Like Sonty, they have several alternatives, including Corel's WordPerfect suite, IBM's Workplace, Apple's iWork, and the free OpenOffice program, increasingly popular with governments determined to bring Microsoft to heel. Plus, there's a host of free online offerings such as Google Spreadsheets and ajaxWrite, which appeal to youngsters not already hooked on Microsoft products.

GENERATION GAPS

Nobody expects Microsoft to collapse under this assault. Most users will figure it's easier to upgrade than to switch from Office, and the streets of techdom are littered with tattered companies that went up against Office and lost. Still, there's the potential for a flowering of choices for PC users. "People are dissatisfied with the status quo," says analyst Jason Maynard of Credit Suisse. "Who knows if you can break the monopoly, but if we see some innovation, there could be some big changes."

For years, Office's toughest competition has been, well, older versions of Office. Typically, when Microsoft releases a new version, up to 50% of its customers are still using the version from two generations earlier. The company has tried to encourage adoption by offering businesses multiyear contracts that include upgrade rights. But the results have been none too scintillating. According to an October, 2005, survey by market researcher Gartner Inc, Office 2003 represented just 45% of the installed base of customers that signed those contracts. And for companies that didn't sign up, it accounted for just 2%. This ho-hum attitude shows why sales of Office and related products are expected by Credit Suisse to grow a sluggish 5% this fiscal year. Such is Microsoft's frustration that last year it risked offending customers with a series of ads portraying those who don't upgrade as dinosaurs.

In an effort to gin up demand for the upcoming release, Microsoft has simplified navigation of the programs and improved the "help" function. If a PC user passes the cursor over an icon in Excel, for instance, it launches a little demonstration of how that feature can be used. "We're doing some amazing reinventions of our product to get people to see that there's a lot of new value we can deliver," says Chris Capossela, a Microsoft corporate vice-president.

For people who don't crave the latest bells and whistles, however, OpenOffice can be good enough. It's a clone of Office—meaning that it works similarly and that documents made with one set of programs can be viewed in the other. In four years the software has been downloaded more than 40 million times. While the main draw is for individuals, some large businesses and government agencies are trying it: Banco do Brasil, one of that country's largest banks, has it loaded on 35,000 PCs.

So far, OpenOffice hasn't put much of a dent in Microsoft's market share. That's partly because while its basic word processor documents and spreadsheets are compatible with Microsoft's, more complex spreadsheets and some slide show presentations created in Office can't be viewed properly in OpenOffice.

But that could change. In May, the International Organization for Standardization approved a new technology standard, the Open Document Format, that's designed to assure that any word processor or spreadsheet application using it can communicate freely with any other. Governments, including Massachusetts' executive branch, have decided to adopt the standard. That means no one company—namely Microsoft—will hold the key to being able to look at all of their documents into perpetuity. So far, the standard has been adopted by OpenOffice, Workplace, and some of the new online software packages. "We don't want to be forced to upgrade, and we want more competition," says Louis Gutierrez, Massachusetts' chief information officer. Microsoft is fighting back. It has come out with its own new file format, which it pledges to license for free to all comers. Microsoft hopes to get approval from the standards group within 18 months. If it does, there will be two competing document format standards— which, some government officials say, would defeat the purpose of having a standard in the first place.

WOOING YOUTH

While governments and businesses face all sorts of hurdles if they want to switch from Office, consumers have little holding them back. To try out the latest online applications, all they need to do is point a Web browser at one of the many Web sites offering them. Take ajaxWrite, the first of a series of applications coming from startup Ajax13 Inc. The company's goal is to take the essential functions of Office to the online world—and add Web collaboration. It is a clear play for younger users. "They're the ones who are familiar with the online world. They don't need a box to hug," says Ajax13 Chief Executive Michael Robertson. Analysts expect Microsoft to create its own online applications if demand emerges.

Over time, the software world is expected to move more to online applications. Gartner considers them a serious threat to Office just because they're so easy to use. "For consumers, I don't think you need to pay the premium to buy Microsoft Office anymore," says Credit Suisse's Maynard.

Further down the road, some techies believe productivity applications as we know them will become much less important. Instead of opening separate word processors and spreadsheets, people may tap into those functions within other applications—much as they now use a word processor within their e-mail programs. If that happens, Microsoft Office, rather than the company's customers, will look like the dinosaur.

Things to Think About

1. What alternatives to Office are in the marketplace? What is the market share for Office? What has been Office's toughest competition thus far? Explain.

2. Why is OpenOffice described as a clone to Microsoft's Office? What would you consider the weaknesses of adopting OpenOffice over Microsoft's Office? Why might that change?

3. How is government encouraging competition in the Office software market? How is Microsoft fighting back? Does government have a right to act in a way that influences competition?

4. Do you expect that Microsoft will move to online applications? Why would this be expected to be a serious threat to Office? How are younger users affected?

5. Do you agree with those who believe that Office may become integrated as part of other programs? Explain. Give an example of such a program.

Key Words

1. GOOG

2. OpenOffice

FORUM 11

Instructional Technology

Article Overview

Nicholas Negroponte, the founding Chairman of the MIT Media Lab, the keynote speaker at the National Education Computing Conference in San Diego in July of 2006, was greeted with enthusiasm by educators nationwide. He spoke of his work as the co-founder of One Laptop Per Child (OLPC), designed for poor children living in remote areas of the world. The laptop, designed to help close the digital divide globally, will utilize the Linux operating system, hold a 500 MHz processor, 128 MB DRAM, 500MB Flash memory, four USB ports, and wireless broadband. It now appears that Negroponte's work may have promoted competition. Instead of promoting individual processing power per computer, an alternative to consider may be a thin client architecture at an even lower cost. This new client computer is designed to be especially small so that the bulk of the processing occurs on the server. Is it a better solution than Negroponte's? Is it rather a different solution for a different market?

Article: *Company touts thin-client solution as viable alternative with few drawbacks*

By COREY MURRAY
September 22, 2006
eSchool News

As education technology advocates await the release of Nicholas Negroponte's $100 laptop, a South Korean technology start-up believes is has developed a solution that can provide students the full experience of one-to-one computing without the drawbacks or limitations of a bargain-basement machine. What's more, they contend, it can be done for less.

September 22, 2006—As educators worldwide await the release of Nicholas Negroponte's $100 laptop and technology luminaries such as Bill Gates and others continue to predict a future dominated by affordable technologies destined to change the face of learning in the 21st century, a fledgling tech company says it has created a solution capable of delivering the benefits of a fully functional PC to every student—today.

The kicker: They can do it for less than $100 a student, says Stephen Dukker, chairman and CEO of nComputing, whose company manufactures a suite of products that promise to turn a single computer or server into an interconnected network of as many as 30 machines.

Rather than provide students with their own CPU, the technology operates similar to a thin-client solution, enabling users to do everything from create standard word-processing documents and spreadsheets to watch streaming video and use complex multimedia, all reportedly without compromising the speed and overall functionality of the other machines connected to the network.

So far, Dukker says, response from the education community to the product has been overwhelming. Though the product line doesn't celebrate its official launch until Sept. 25, he noted, the company already has shipped some 12,000 units to U.S. schools, with more than 100,000 going to customers in developing nations.

How do they do it?

In a meeting with *eSchool News* editors Sept. 21, Dukker demonstrated how the product works by connecting to a host computer and feeding off an existing CPU. Resembling a standard memory card, the device can be installed inside an existing machine, where it branches out via standard Ethernet cables to a network of satellite keyboards and monitors, fueling the computing needs of up to seven users off the processing power of a single machine. If customers prefer not to load the cards (each card supports up to three users) inside existing CPUs, nComputing also provides a version of the same card that comes housed in its own stand-alone box. Additional users then connect to the satellite box, which is linked to the host machine or server.

Unlike Negroponte's prototype device, which contains its own processor and operates as a scaled-down version of a traditional laptop computer, nComputing's device isn't a computer at all, explains Dukker.

Not unlike the human brain, Dukker says, most personal computers eat up only a very small portion of their overall processing power when in use. Rather than up production costs by purchasing expensive processors from leading chip makers such as Intel and AMD, he said, the company found it could drastically reduce its costs to users by designing a device that simply borrowed its processing power from existing PCs. The finished product has no operating system, runs zero software applications, and uses about as much energy as a household light bulb; but, when paired with a another machine, Dukker says, it provides users with a near- seamless computing experience, limited only by the output of its host.

The idea, he explains, is to give users a product that allows them to take full advantage of the computing power they've already been forced to buy.

In the IT business, everything is driven by cost," says Dukker, who before joining nComputing was founder and CEO of eMachines, a low-cost computer manufacturer recently acquired by Gateway.

Where the bar for affordable, one-to-one computing in schools was set by Negroponte's $100 prototype, Dukker says his company is capable of driving those costs down to as low as $70 a seat, a figure he believes will fall even further as production costs for materials drop.

In the case of Negroponte's solution, Dukker said, "it really all goes back to that old problem of trying to stuff 10 pounds of parts into a five-pound bag."

While the $100 laptop could very well spark an education revolution in some third-world nations, Dukker says, educators in economically advanced countries, including the U.S., likely won't be satisfied with their ability to perform only basic tasks such as word processing and eMail.

In an age where the phrase "21st century skills" has become a mantra for schools looking to better prepare students for the challenges of a new world economy, Dukker says, educators and students today demand more from their machines.

Apart from completing simple tasks, Dukker demonstrated how nComputing's product—when connected to a host computer—could perform more intensive, multimedia-type functions such as streaming internet video, while still maintaining near-seamless integration and image quality.

The company also has developed a web-based interface designed to help educators and others better manage and communicate with networked users. Loaded onto the host computer, NControl software enables educators to view and manipulate the screens of their students, creating an environment that is both interactive and controlled. The software reportedly works not only in single classroom environments, but also across entire networks, wherever networked users are located.

Compatible with host machines running Windows or Linux-based operating systems, the latest terminal boxes boast additional USB and serial ports, enabling students to save their information to a portable device they can then take with them as they move through the building. Because the terminals borrow their power from a single source, users eventually might run into problems when trying to run processor-heavy applications, such as the latest computer games. But, at least where schools are concerned, Dukker said, most of the applications used in a typical education environment should run unencumbered.

While the $70-a-seat price quoted by Dukker is already being realized in select districts, some circumstances could drive the cost to schools higher.

Where schools use Windows-based machines, for example, district administrators will want to check with Microsoft to ensure that the terminals can legally serve multiple users off a single licensing agreement. Though this is a non-issue with Linux-based machines, schools running on a Microsoft platform need to be conscious of the possibility of random software audits and pricing concerns that stand to drive the price of the deployment higher.

nComputing says its products are intended to reduce hardware deployment and maintenance costs and that it does not provide specific guidance to schools with regards to licensing, but that it encourages schools to check first with their software vendors.

"There are many possible configurations and uses for the NStation products and many possible combinations of software and license terms that may apply to a user's host computer," wrote an nComputing spokesperson in an eMail response to *eSchool News*. "Whether additional software licenses are required may depend upon an organization's particular configuration and use of the NStation products, the operating system software, and other software on the host computer, and the particular licenses that apply to that software."

Total cost of ownership, or TCO, is another long-standing issue the company believes its product should enable schools to improve upon.

"One of the attributes that our customers absolutely love is that these devices are never obsolete," said Dukker.

Because each terminal is powered by a host, schools need only upgrade their host machines, or servers, in order to refresh their network. The result is that technicians can spend less time performing routine maintenance and concentrate more on improving other network efficiencies, he said.

Depending on what customers are looking for, however, the product does have some drawbacks. For one, unlike Negroponte's device—which is wireless and can be used in classrooms that don't have sufficient electrical power—nComputing's solution is hard-wired and requires a viable power source.

And though the company estimates it can provide a full computing experience at less than $70 a seat, in many cases, the cost of monitors and other add-ons likely will drive the final price for schools even higher.

Still, Dukker likes his chances. While the product only recently became available to U.S. schools, he said, it has history of success in the international community.

In 2005, at a conference in Hanover, Germany, the company won a CeBIT award for best server-based application. And last December, the World Trade Organization tapped nComputing to provide Pentium 4-style computing power to all of its participants at an annual meeting in Hong Kong.

In Mexico, one customer reportedly used the technology to create a portable internet cafe in the back of a truck. In China, the mayor of one rural village set up a shared internet connection for other members of his community. And in Thailand, educators at schools and universities are experimenting with the product.

Rather than wait years to get Negroponte's device, which will be deployed in advance to developing nations before being made available to schools in the United States, or hang around until Gates finally settles on a prototype that suits his tastes, a number of U.S. schools already have decided to give nComputing shot.

One of those school systems—the Nash Rocky Mountain School District in North Carolina—decided after testing the product for one month to order $50,000 worth of devices to be installed and deployed throughout the district.

The same can be said for Fremont Joint School District in St. Anthony, Idaho.

"It gets viral," said Dukker, talking about how word-of-mouth has generated sales in neighboring rural districts throughout the Midwest.

His hope is that schools will at least consider their options.

Things to Think About

1. Can nComputing's device be compared to grid computing technology? Explain.

2. Why does Dukker suggest that his device is not a computer at all? Describe the device.

3. Explain the comparison Dukker makes between the processing unit of a computer and the human brain.

4. Explain how Dukker and Negroponte differ in the way they have chosen to reduce costs in their designs. Dukker suggests that the two serve different markets. Explain. Do you agree with Dukker's assertion? Do you agree with Dukker's argument that Negroponte's machine will not satisfy most consumers in the United States?

5. How will NControl software be utilized?

Key Terms

1. TCO

2. Prototype

FORUM 12

Intellectual Property Rights

Article Overview

When the subject matter is a product of the mind or the intellect, it is identified as intellectual property. In law, there are legal entitlements for intellectual property that entitle the owner to exclusive rights. Reminiscent of Google's interest in digitizing copyrighted books, McLean High School plans to add student essays to the database used by a for-profit service company to determine if the students engaged in plagiarism. Do the students have a case?

Article: *Students Rebel Against Database Designed to Thwart Plagiarists*

By MARIA GLOD
September 22, 2006
The Washington Post; p. A01

When McLean High School students write this year about Othello or immigration policy, their teachers won't be the only ones examining the papers. So will a California company that specializes in catching cheaters.

The for-profit service known as Turnitin checks student work against a database of more than 22 million papers written by students around the world, as well as online sources and electronic archives of journals. School administrators said the service, which they will start using next week, is meant to deter plagiarism at a time when the Internet makes it easy to copy someone else's words.

But some McLean High students are rebelling. Members of the new Committee for Students' Rights said they do not cheat or condone cheating. But they object to Turnitin's automatically adding their essays to the massive database, calling it an infringement of intellectual property rights. And they contend that the school's action will tar students at one of Fairfax County's academic powerhouses.

"It irked a lot of people because there's an implication of assumed guilt," said Ben Donovan, 18, a senior who helped collect 1,190 student signatures on a petition against mandatory use of the service. "It's like if you searched every car in the parking lot or drug-tested every student."

Questions about the legality and effectiveness of plagiarism detection services such as Turnitin are swirling beyond McLean High, another sign of the challenge educators face as they navigate benefits and problems the Internet has brought.

Fairfax school and Turnitin officials said lawyers for the company and various universities have concluded that the paper-checking system does not violate student rights. Many educators agree. Turnitin, a leader in the field, lists Georgetown University and the University of Maryland's University College among its clients. Others include some public schools in Montgomery, Prince George's, Loudoun and Arlington counties.

But three professors at Grand Valley State University in Michigan this month posted a letter online arguing that Turnitin "makes questionable use of student intellectual property." The University of Kansas last week decided to let its contract with Turnitin expire because of cost and intellectual property concerns. And the intellectual property caucus of the Conference on College Composition and Communication, an organization of 6,000 college-level educators, is debating whether such services "undermine students' authority over the uses of their own writing" and make them feel "guilty until proven innocent," according to a draft position statement.

"There's a lot of debate out there," said Rebecca Ingalls, a University of Tampa English professor who has analyzed Turnitin. "These students are giving their work to a company that's making money and they are getting no compensation."

Kimberly Carney, an assistant principal at McLean High, said there have been isolated cases of plagiarism at the 1,770-student school. The main reason administrators will use Turnitin is to teach students how to give proper credit to sources, Carney said.

"There wasn't a landmark thing that happened that we said we need to adopt this," Carney said. "Plagiarism is a problem at every high school nationwide."

The Fairfax County system began using Turnitin in 2003. More than three-fourths of the county's high schools now use the service.

The Center for Academic Integrity, affiliated with Duke University's Kenan Institute for Ethics, surveyed 18,000 public and private high school students over four years and found that more than 60 percent admitted to some form of plagiarism, according to a 2005 report.

Turnitin charges about 80 cents per student per year, according to a company official. Fairfax County paid between $24,000 and $30,000 in the last school year for the service, school system officials said.

Founder John M. Barrie said Turnitin evolved out of a Web site he created to facilitate peer review when he was a graduate student at the University of California at Berkeley. When fellow students complained about cheating classmates, Barrie helped develop a system to catch them. Turnitin's parent company, iParadigms LLC, of Oakland, Calif., was launched 10 years ago.

The service has grown dramatically, Barrie said, and is now used by more than 6,000 academic institutions in 90 countries. Barrie, who is president and chief executive of iParadigms, said 60,000 student assignments are added to the database daily. He said no student has ever launched a legal challenge.

Barrie said Turnitin helps protect the interests of honest students. The database is used only to compare papers, he said. "None of our clients want to catch cheaters," he said. "They all want to deter cheaters. Just like a proctor in an SAT exam or like a referee on a football field."

Dan Kent, a Loudoun County social studies teacher, called Turnitin necessary in a "cut-and-paste world." When Kent became department chair at Ashburn's Broad Run High School in 1999, he said, many teachers were reluctant to assign complex research papers because of the difficulty they encountered in checking for plagiarism.

These days, many Loudoun students submit rough drafts to Turnitin. They receive an "originality report" that identifies similarities to other sources and alerts the student and teacher. Teachers then eyeball the paper and decide if the material is properly cited.

Broad Run uncovered three instances of serious plagiarism in the first year it used Turnitin, Kent said, and other cases of poor paraphrasing that students failed to recognize as inappropriate. Since 2002, he said, the service has rooted out only three additional plagiarism cases at the school.

Carney said McLean High will use a similar approach. Students will be allowed to submit unlimited numbers of drafts to the service to catch intentional or accidental overlaps. Only the final version will be graded. Students who refuse to use Turnitin will be given a zero on the assignment.

Carney predicted that McLean students would embrace the system eventually. "They'll see it's not a 'gotcha,' " she said.

But members of the Committee for Students' Rights want the school to allow students to opt out. In an interview at a Starbucks near the campus, they said that they can learn about plagiarism directly from teachers and that there are other ways to catch cheaters. They also said fees paid to Turnitin would be better spent on other educational matters.

"McLean is a great school," said Nicholas Kaylor, 17, a senior. "They should have a little bit of trust in us."

Things to Think About

1. Is an ethical dilemma present in regard to the loss of intellectual property rights in order to avoid the theft of another's property? Are the students guilty until proven innocent? What are your thoughts on the legality of the issue?

2. At about $30,000 a year for one school system, is the service cost effective? Could it be better spent in other areas?

3. Does Kent's experience with the service bode well for others?

4. Specifically, how is the service utilized?

5. Do you believe that students will eventually embrace the service, as Carney suggests? What is the position of the Committee for Students' Rights? Explain.

Key Terms

1. Intellectual Property Rights

2. Originality Report

FORUM 13

Electronic Background Searches

Article Overview

With MySpace recently replacing Google and Yahoo as the top U.S. Web site, users take heed that employers are including social web sites as part of their online research used to avoid costly hiring mistakes. Employers are visiting the site to search for insights into prospective employees' judgments and behaviors. What information do you make available? What information does government make available?

Article: *Face It: 'Book' No Secret to Employer*

By JACQUELINE PALANK
July 17, 2006
The Washington Times

At least one Washington intern is glad she did not post unprofessional information about herself on the social-networking Web site Facebook: A potential employer asked a past intern to look up her profile.

Started in February 2004 as a Web site for college students to list their interests, communicate with friends and meet people, Facebook now boasts more than 8 million registered members from universities, high schools and workplaces across the country.

As the popularity of Facebook, MySpace and other social-networking Web sites grows, employers are signing up and logging in to perform background checks on job and internship candidates, or asking employees who are members to do so.

"The Internet's fair game," said the intern, an upcoming junior at Barnard College who asked not to be named because she didn't want to identify the D.C. nonprofit think tank that looked up her posting. She turned down the position offered, she said, but not because of the employer's actions.

The intern said she created her Facebook profile fully aware of the Internet's public nature.

"There were no pictures of me drunk on the floor in the bathroom," she said. "I feel it's like checking a reference. You just want to make sure you look good."

A poll released last week found that 26.9 percent of employers check the backgrounds of job applicants by using Google and social-networking Web sites. The National Association of Colleges and Employers surveyed 254 organizations in the services, manufacturing and government-nonprofit sectors.

Of the employers who said they use Web sites, 41.2 percent reported occasional use, 35.3 percent said their use was infrequent and 7.4 percent called it standard practice.

MySpace replaced Yahoo and Google as the top U.S. Web site last week and garnered 80 percent of all visits to social-networking Web sites, Reuters news agency reported Tuesday, citing figures from Internet tracking firm Hitwise. Facebook received the second-highest number of visits to social-networking sites, a distant 7.6 percent.

Though employers often deny using search engines or looking up profiles, "they do it all day long," said Tim DeMello, founder and chief executive of Ziggs, a Boston company that creates free online professional profiles and, for a fee, uses search terms to place the profiles at the top of 20 search engines' results. He said the average Ziggs profile receives 28 clicks a month.

"Whether you like it or not, employers can sit down in the quiet confines of their office, go on the Web and get information on someone," Mr. DeMello said.

Mr. DeMello, who uses search engines and social-networking sites to check on job applicants, said recent college graduates are more likely to be found through social-networking sites than search engines. He said such sites demonstrate the level of the job applicant's judgment and give employers insight into their personality.

Fairfax County Public Schools requires that every job applicant complete an employee background information form, be fingerprinted and undergo a criminal background check, spokeswoman Mary Shaw said. Google may be used for some candidates.

It's not the first thing we do, and it's not for everyone, but [we would use Google] if something comes up that might give us pause before we extend the job offer," Ms. Shaw said.

Postings on social-networking sites are not limited to a circle of friends, but "the young people who put up information there think that it's private," said Marva Gumbs Jennings, executive director of the George Washington University Career Center.

Even the privacy settings on Facebook and MySpace might not protect a job candidate. A friend with access to the profile and photographs could provide the information at an employer's request. Mrs. Gumbs Jennings said there is a way to access any information posted.

Mrs. Gumbs Jennings suggests to users of such sites: If you don't want to see information on the front page of a newspaper, don't publish it online.

"You only have one chance to make a good first impression," said Nancy Ahlrichs, president of EOC Strategies, which helps companies recruit and retain top-notch employees. "Because it is open to scrutiny, once you know you're going to launch a job search, you might want to clean up what's out there."

Things to Think About

1. How many employers have reported using social networking sites to check the backgrounds of their employees? If you were in a hiring capacity, would you use web site for this purpose? Would it present an ethical dilemma for you?

2. Do privacy settings absolutely protect a job candidate? Explain.

3. Do most consumers now recognize that the Internet is fair game?

4. Does government utilize search engines and social networking sites to research employees? Which site obtained the second highest rate of hits?

5. What advice do Jennings and Ahlrichs give prospective employees? Can you add to this?

Key Terms

1. Hitwise

2. Ziggs

FORUM 14

Electronic Election Systems

Article Overview

Is the fundamental right to vote and be counted jeopardized by technology? With 40% of Americans expected to vote on a computer in the next election, the threat of malicious software manipulating vote tallies is of great concern to the electorate. Since Princeton University researchers have recently exposed large vulnerabilities in the voting machines, what responsive actions should follow?

Article: *The Big Gamble on Electronic Voting*

By RANDALL STROSS
September 24, 2006
Digital Domain

HANGING chads made it difficult to read voter intentions in 2000. Hotel minibar keys may do the same for the elections in November.

The mechanics of voting have undergone a major change since the imbroglio that engulfed presidential balloting in 2000. Embarrassed by an election that had to be settled by the Supreme Court, Congress passed the Help America Vote Act of 2002, which provided funds to improve voting equipment.

From 2003 to 2005, some $3 billion flew out of the federal purse for equipment purchases. Nothing said "state of the art" like a paperless voting machine that electronically records and tallies votes with the tap of a touch screen. Election Data Services, a political consulting firm that specializes in redistricting, estimates that about 40 percent of registered voters will use an electronic machine in the coming elections.

One brand of machine leads in market share by a sizable margin: the AccuVote, made by Diebold Election Systems. Two weeks ago, however, Diebold suffered one of the worst kinds of public embarrassment for a company that began in 1859 by making safes and vaults.

Edward W. Felten, a professor of computer science at Princeton, and his student collaborators conducted a demonstration with an AccuVote TS and noticed that the key to the machine's memory card slot appeared to be similar to one that a staff member had at home.

When he brought the key into the office and tried it, the door protecting the AccuVote's memory card slot swung open obligingly. Upon examination, the key turned out to be a standard industrial part used in simple locks for office furniture, computer cases, jukeboxes — and hotel minibars.

Once the memory card slot was accessible, how difficult would it be to introduce malicious software that could manipulate vote tallies? That is one of the questions that Professor Felten and two of his students, Ariel J. Feldman and J. Alex Haldeman, have been investigating. In the face of Diebold's refusal to let scientists test the AccuVote, the Princeton team got its hands on a machine only with the help of a third party.

Even before the researchers had made the serendipitous discovery about the minibar key, they had released a devastating critique of the AccuVote's security. For computer scientists, they supplied a technical paper; for the general public, they prepared an accompanying video. Their short answer to the question of the practicality of vote theft with the AccuVote: easily accomplished.

The researchers demonstrated the machine's vulnerability to an attack by means of code that can be introduced with a memory card. The program they devised does not tamper with the voting process. The machine records each vote as it should, and makes a backup copy, too.

Every 15 seconds or so, however, the rogue program checks the internal vote tallies, then adds and subtracts votes, as needed, to reach programmed targets; it also makes identical changes in the backup file. The alterations cannot be detected later because the total number of votes perfectly matches the total number of voters. At the end of the election day, the rogue program erases itself, leaving no trace.

On Sept. 13, when Princeton's Center for Information Technology Policy posted its findings, Diebold issued a press release that shrugged off the demonstration and analysis. It said Princeton's AccuVote machine was "two generations old" and "not used anywhere in the country."

I spoke last week with Professor Felten, who said he could not imagine how a newer version of the AccuVote's software could protect itself against this kind of attack. But he also said he would welcome the opportunity to test it. I called Diebold to see if it would lend Princeton a machine.

Mark G. Radke, director for marketing at Diebold, said that the AccuVote machines were certified by state election officials and that no academic researcher would be permitted to test an AccuVote supplied by the company. "This is analogous to launching a nuclear missile," he said enigmatically, adding that Diebold had to restrict "access to the buttons."

I persisted. Suppose, I asked, that a test machine were placed in the custodial care of the United States Election Assistance Commission, a government agency. Mr. Radke demurred again, saying the company's critics were so focused on software that they "have no appreciation of physical security" that protects the machines from intrusion.

This same point was featured prominently in the company's press release that criticized the Princeton study, saying it "all but ignores physical security and election procedures." It is a criticism that collides with the facts on Page 5 of the Princeton study, where the authors provide step-by-step details of how to install the malicious software in the AccuVote.

Even before the minibar lineage of the AccuVote key had been discovered, the researchers had learned that the lock was easily circumvented: one of them could consistently pick it in less than 10 seconds.

If skeptics cannot believe what they read about the ease of manipulating an election, they can watch the 10-minute online video: the AccuVote lock is picked, a memory card is inserted and the malicious software is loaded; the machine is rebooted, and within 60 seconds the machine is ready to throw the election in favor of any specified candidate.

Computer scientists with expertise in security issues have been sounding alarms for years. David L. Dill at Stanford and Douglas W. Jones at the University of Iowa were among the first to alert the public to potential problems. But the possibility of vote theft by electronic means remained nothing more than a hypothesis — until the summer of 2003, when the code for the AccuVote's operating system was discovered on a Diebold server that was publicly accessible.

The code quickly made its way into researchers' hands. Suspected vulnerabilities were confirmed, and never-contemplated sloppiness was added to the list of concerns. At a computer security conference, the AccuVote's anatomy was analyzed closely by a team: Aviel D. Rubin, a computer science professor at Johns Hopkins; two junior associates, Tadayoshi Kohno and Adam Stubblefield; and Dan S. Wallach, an associate professor in computer science at Rice. They described how the AccuVote software design rendered the machine vulnerable to manipulation by smart cards. They found that the standard protections to prevent alteration of the internal code were missing; they characterized the system as "far below even the most minimal security standards."

Professor Rubin has just published a nontechnical memoir, "Brave New Ballot: The Battle to Safeguard Democracy in the Age of Electronic Voting" (Morgan Road Books), that describes how his quiet life was upended after he and his colleagues published their paper. He recalls in his book that Diebold's lawyers sent each of the paper's authors a letter threatening the possibility of legal action, warning them to "exercise caution" in interviews with the press lest they make a statement that would "appear designed to improperly impair and impede Diebold's existing and future business." Johns Hopkins rallied to his side, however, and the university's president, William R. Brody, commended him for being on the case.

Recently, there have been signs that states are having second thoughts about trusting their AccuVote equipment. Officials in California, Florida and Pennsylvania have been outspoken about their concerns. In Maryland earlier this year, the state House of Delegates voted 137 to 0 in favor of a bill to prohibit the use of its AccuVote machines because they were not equipped to generate a paper audit trail. (The state Senate did not take up the measure and it died.)

Professor Rubin favors the use of touch screens only for "ballot marking" — capturing a voter's intended choice — then printing out a paper ballot with only the voter's chosen candidates that the voter can visually check. Election officials can then use the slip to tally votes with an optical scanner made by a different manufacturer.

Manual audits of the tallies in at least 1 percent of all precincts, as is now required in California, would provide a transparent method of checking for integrity. Should a full recount be necessary, the paper ballots, containing only the selected names, provide unambiguous records of original intent.

"Let computers do what they do best," Professor Rubin said, "and let paper do what it does best."

Randall Stross is an author based in Silicon Valley and a professor of business at San Jose State University. E-mail: digitaldomain@nytimes.com.

Things to Think About

1. How was Diebold recently publicly embarrassed? Explain.

2. Why did Diebold refuse to let scientists test the AccuVote?

3. Even before the Princeton test, the AccuVote had problems. Explain.

4. Do you agree with Diebold's defense? Explain.

5. Why did Diebold threaten legal action against Prof. Rubin? What backlash has the experiment had on the state level? Manual audits of the tallies in at least 1% of all precincts are now required in California. Should this be implemented nationwide?

Key Terms

1. AccuVote

2. Help America Vote Act of 2002

FORUM 15

Laser Technology

Article Overview

M oore's Law was an observation made in 1965 by Gordon Moore, co-founder of Intel, that the number of transistors per square inch on integrated circuits had doubled every year since the integrated circuit was invented, increasing processing speed and diminishing costs. In recent years, data density has doubled every eighteen months, which is the current definition, and it is predicted that it will continue to do so for the next two decades. Now it appears that the data communications industry will be on the same curve. A silicon-based chip can now produce laser beams, using laser light rather than wires to send data between chips.

Article: *A Chip That Can Transfer Data Using Laser Light*

By JOHN MARKOFF
September 18, 2006
The New York Times

SAN FRANCISCO, Sept. 17 — Researchers plan to announce on Monday that they have created a silicon-based chip that can produce laser beams. The advance will make it possible to use laser light rather than wires to send data between chips, removing the most significant bottleneck in computer design.

As a result, chip makers may be able to put the high-speed data communications industry on the same curve of increased processing speed and diminishing costs — the phenomenon known as Moore's law — that has driven the computer industry for the last four decades.

The development is a result of research at Intel, the world's largest chip maker, and the University of California, Santa Barbara. Commercializing the new technology may not happen before the end of the decade, but the prospect of being able to place hundreds or thousands of data-carrying light beams on standard industry chips is certain to shake up both the communications and computer industries.

Lasers are already used to transmit high volumes of computer data over longer distances — for example, between offices, cities and across oceans — using fiber optic cables. But in computer chips, data moves at great speed over the wires inside, then slows to a snail's pace when it is sent chip-to-chip inside a computer.

With the barrier removed, computer designers will be able to rethink computers, packing chips more densely both in home systems and in giant data centers. Moreover, the laser-silicon chips — composed of a spider's web of laser light in addition to metal wires — portend a vastly more powerful and less expensive national computing infrastructure. For a few dollars apiece, such chips could transmit data at 100 times the speed of laser-based communications equipment, called optical transceivers, that typically cost several thousand dollars.

Currently fiber optic networks are used to transmit data to individual neighborhoods in cities where the data is then distributed by slower conventional wire-based communications gear. The laser chips will make it possible to send avalanches of data to and from individual homes at far less cost.

They could also give rise to a new class of supercomputers that could share data internally at speeds not possible today.

The breakthrough was achieved by bonding a layer of light-emitting indium phosphide onto the surface of a standard silicon chip etched with special channels that act as light-wave guides. The resulting sandwich has the potential to create on a computer chip hundreds and possibly thousands of tiny, bright lasers that can be switched on and off billions of times a second.

"This is a field that has just begun exploding in the past 18 months," said Eli Yablonovitch, a physicist at the University of California, Los Angeles, a leading researcher in the field. "There is going to be a lot more optical communications in computing than people have thought."

Indeed, the results of the development work, which will be reported in a coming issue of Optics Express, an international journal, indicate that a high-stakes race is under way worldwide. While the researchers at Intel and Santa Barbara are betting on indium phosphide, Japanese scientists in a related effort are pursuing a different material, the chemical element erbium.

Although commercial chips with built-in lasers are years away, Luxtera, a company in Carlsbad, Calif., is already selling test chips that incorporate most optical components directly into silicon and then inject laser light from a separate source.

The Intel-Santa Barbara work proves that it is possible to make complete photonic devices using standard chip-making machinery, although not entirely out of silicon. "There has always been this final hurdle," said Mario Paniccia, director of the Photonics Technology Lab at Intel. "We have now come up with a solution that optimizes both sides."

In the past it has proved impossible to couple standard silicon with the exotic materials that emit light when electrically charged. But the university team supplied a low-temperature bonding technique that does not melt the silicon circuitry. The approach uses an electrically charged oxygen gas to create a layer of oxide just 25 atoms thick on each material. When heated and pressed together, the oxide layer fuses the two materials into a single chip that conducts information both through wires and on beams of reflected light.

"Photonics has been a low-volume cottage industry," said John E. Bowers, director of the Multidisciplinary Optical Switching Technology Center at the University of California,

Santa Barbara. "Everything will change and laser communications will be everywhere, including fiber to the home."

Photonics industry experts briefed on the technique said that it would almost certainly pave the way for commercialization of the long-sought convergence of silicon chips and optical lasers. "Before, there was more hype than substance," said Alan Huang, a former Bell Laboratories researcher who is a pioneer in the field and is now chief technology officer of the Terabit Corporation, a photonics start-up company in Menlo Park, Calif. "Now I believe this will lead to future applications in optoelectronics."

Things to Think About

1. When can we expect laser light to send data between computer chips on a commercial basis? How do we use laser now to transmit high volumes of data. Explain the difference.

2. How will this development impact cost?

3. Describe how the breakthrough was achieved. Is optical communications an avenue for technologists to consider?

4. How will computer designers be able to rethink computers? How do you envision your environment fifty years from now?

5. Explain how data is transmitted through fiber optic networks now.

Key Terms

1. Photonics

2. Optoelectronics

FORUM 16

Malware

Article Overview

President George Bush called for a "new ethic of responsibility" in corporate America in 2002. The Sarbanes –Oxley Act followed to impose responsibility on industry, management and employees to safeguard information. Finally, the National Strategy to Secure Cyberspace was released in 2003 to create public and private cooperation to regulate and defend the national computer networks from hazards like viruses. What does the data suggest in regards to our efforts?

Article: *Beware of Malware on Social Sites*

By MAXIM KELLY
August 9, 2006
ElectricNews.net

Social networking sites are behind a surge of viruses, spyware and other 'nasty stuff', according to web security firm ScanSafes's monthly report.

According to an analysis of more than 5 billion web requests in July, ScanSafe found that on average, up to one in 600 profile pages on social networking sites hosted some form of malware.

The company also reported that the use of social networking sites, often assumed to be popular only amongst teens, accounted for approximately 1 percent of all internet use in the workplace.

"Social networking sites have been newsworthy because of the concern over our children's safety, but beyond unsafe contact with harmful adults, these sites are an emerging and potentially ripe threat vector that can expose children to harmful software," said Eldar Tuvey, chief executive and co-founder of ScanSafe. "Users are frequently subject to unwanted spyware and adware that can compromise their PCs, track online behaviour and degrade PC performance," he said.

The majority of malware identified by ScanSafe was spyware and adware, and ranged from the more benign programs that track usage to difficult-to-remove spyware which may redirect a user to dodgy websites.

Social networking sites like Facebook, which typically use a university or college e-mail address to verify a user's identity, and LinkedIn, a site used for business networking, tended to be more secure than "open" social networking sites, according to ScanSafe.

The research also revealed the presence of referrals to adult-themed dating sites on social network sites popular with teens.

"The presence of adult-oriented adware is disturbing, not only because much of it is inappropriate content for minors, but because underage users may not be in a position to consent to installing adware or understand the end-user licence agreement," Tuvey said.

In addition to the statistics on social networking sites, ScanSafe reported that overall spyware increased 19 percent in July while web viruses decreased 14 percent. Web viruses identified and blocked by ScanSafe before a virus' signature (i.e. the code which antivirus software uses to identify it) became available accounted for nearly 13 percent of all web viruses blocked by the company in July.

Tuvey commented that there may be some seasonality to web viruses and spyware but the number of unidentified viruses remains relatively constant.

The ScanSafe Global Threat Centre processed more than 5 billion web requests in July, and reported that it blocked 238 unique viruses — 75 of which were new or unique viruses.

Things to Think About

1. What does the surge of viruses over social networking sites suggest about the accountability of the management of the sites themselves?

2. Does the proliferation of viruses on these sites suggest that consumers are not securing their own computers?

3. What measures could be implemented to assist consumers to secure their computers?

4. What is Tuvey's greatest concern regarding adware on social networking sites? Do you agree? Explain.

5. How can malware degrade PC performance?

Key Words

1. Malware

2. Virus signature

FORUM 17

Cell Phone Security

===

Article Overview

Mobile phone use is increasing around the world. In the United States, it is now common for individuals to no longer own a land line phone. Since phones are now digital, hold picture files and utilize email and text messaging, it is important to acknowledge security concerns, such as spoofing as a means of spreading viruses, as well as data privacy concerns in the disposal of hardware. Do consumers realize that their phones are now computers?

Article: *Don't Keep Secrets on Cell Phones*

By TED BRIDIS, AP writer
August 30, 2006

WASHINGTON — Selling your old phone once you upgrade to a fancier model can be like handing over your diaries. All sorts of sensitive information pile up inside our cellphones, and deleting it may be more difficult than you think.

A popular practice among sellers, resetting the phone, often means sensitive information appears to have been erased. But it can be resurrected using specialized yet inexpensive software found on the Internet.

The married man's girlfriend sent a text message to his cellphone: His wife was getting suspicious. Perhaps they should cool it for a few days.

"So," she wrote, "I'll talk to u next week."

"You want a break from me? Then fine," he wrote back.

Later, the married man bought a new phone. He sold his old one on eBay, at Internet auction, for $290.

The guys who bought it now know his secret.

The married man had followed the directions in his phone's manual to erase all his information, including lurid exchanges with his lover. But it wasn't enough.

A company, Trust Digital of McLean, Va., bought 10 different phones on eBay this summer to test phone-security tools it sells for businesses. The phones all were fairly sophisticated models capable of working with corporate e-mail systems.

Curious software experts at Trust Digital resurrected information on nearly all the used phones, including the racy exchanges between guarded lovers.

The other phones contained:

- One company's plans to win a multimillion-dollar federal transportation contract.

- E-mails about another firm's $50,000 payment for a software license.

- Bank accounts and passwords.

- Details of prescriptions and receipts for one worker's utility payments.

The recovered information was equal to 27,000 pages — a stack of printouts 8 feet high.

"We found just a mountain of personal and corporate data," said Nick Magliato, Trust Digital's chief executive.

Many of the phones were owned personally by the sellers but crammed with sensitive corporate information, underscoring the blurring of work and home. "They don't come with a warning label that says, 'Be careful.' The data on these phones is very important," Magliato said.

One phone surrendered the secrets of a chief executive at a small technology company in Silicon Valley. It included details of a pending deal with Adobe Systems Inc., and e-mail proposals from a potential Japanese partner:

"If we want to be exclusive distributor in Japan, what kind of business terms you want?" asked the executive in Japan.

Trust Digital surmised that the U.S. chief executive gave his old phone to a former roommate, who used it briefly then sold it for $400 on eBay. Researchers found e-mails covering different periods for both men, who used the same address until recently.

Experts said giving away an old phone is commonplace. Consumers upgrade their cellphones on average about every 18 months.

"Most people toss their phones after they're done; a lot of them give their old phones to family members or friends," said Miro Kazakoff, a researcher at Compete Inc. of Boston who follows mobile phone sales and trends. He said selling a used phone — which sometimes can fetch hundreds of dollars — is increasingly popular.

The 10 phones Trust Digital studied represented popular models from leading manufacturers. All the phones stored information on "flash" memory chips, the same technology found in digital cameras and some music players.

Flash memory is inexpensive and durable. But it is slow to erase information in ways that make it impossible to recover. So manufacturers compensate with methods that erase data less completely but don't make a phone seem sluggish.

Phone manufacturers usually provide instructions for safely deleting a customer's information, but it's not always convenient or easy to find. Research in Motion Ltd. has built into newer Blackberry phones an easy-to-use wipe program.

Palm Inc., which makes the popular Treo phones, puts directions deep within its website for what it calls a "zero out reset." It involves holding down three buttons simultaneously while pressing a fourth tiny button on the back of the phone.

But it's so awkward to do that even Palm says it may take two people. A Palm executive, Joe Fabris, said the company made the process deliberately clumsy because it doesn't want customers accidentally erasing their information.

Trust Digital resurrected erased e-mails and other information from a used Treo phone provided by The Associated Press for a demonstration after it was reset and appeared empty. Once the phone was reset using Palm's awkward "zero-out" technique, no information could be recovered. The AP already used that technique to protect data on its reporters' phones.

"The tools are out there" for hackers and thieves to rummage through deleted data on used phones, Trust Digital's chief technology officer, Norm Laudermilch, said. "It definitely does not take a Ph.D."

Fabris, Palm's director of wireless solutions, said the company may warn customers in an upcoming newsletter about the risks of selling their used phones after AP's inquiries. "It might behoove us to raise this issue," Fabris said.

Dean Olmstead of Fresno, Calif., sold his Treo phone on eBay after using it six months. He didn't know about Palm's instructions to safely delete all his personal information. Now, he's worried.

"I probably should have done that," Olmstead said. "Folks need to know this. I'm hoping my phone goes to a nice person."

Guy Martin of Albuquerque, wasn't as concerned someone will snoop on his secrets. He also sold his Treo phone on eBay and didn't delete his information completely.

"I'm not that kind of valuable person, so I'm not really worried," said Martin, who runs the http://www.imusteat.com website. "I guarantee that three-quarters of the people who buy these phones don't think about this."

Trust Digital found no evidence thieves or corporate spies are routinely buying used phones to mine them for secrets, Magliato said. "I don't think the bad guys have figured this out yet."

President Bush's former cybersecurity adviser, Howard Schmidt, carried up to four phones and e-mail devices — and said he was always careful with them. To sanitize his older Blackberry devices, Schmidt would deliberately type his password incorrectly 11 times, which caused data on them to self-destruct.

"People are just not aware how much they're exposing themselves," Schmidt said. "This is more than something you pick up and talk on. This is your identity. There are people really looking to exploit this."

Executives at Trust Digital agreed to review with AP the information extracted from the used phones on the condition AP would not identify the sellers or their employers. They also showed AP receipts from the Internet auctions in which they bought the 10 phones over the summer for prices between $192 and $400 each.

Trust Digital said it intends to return all the phones to their original owners, and said it kept the recovered personal information on a single computer under lock and disconnected from its corporate network at its headquarters in northern Virginia.

Peiter "Mudge" Zatko, a respected computer security expert, said phone owners should decide whether to auction their used equipment for a few hundred dollars — and risk revealing their secrets — or effectively toss their old phones under a large truck to dispose of them.

What about a case like the Lothario whose affair Trust Digital discovered?

"I'd run over the phone," Zatko said. "Maybe give it an acid bath."

Things to Think About

1. If a cell phone user has deleted the data, how can it be resurrected? Does the same hold true for PCs?

2. How often do consumers upgrade their cell phones? Do you predict that this will change? What evidence do you have?

3. What technology is used in cell phone storage? What are its advantages? Disadvantages?

4. How have manufacturers dealt with this issue? How can they improve? Do they have an ethical responsibility to address the issue? How?

5. How pervasive is this problem for those who sell cell phones?

Key Words

1. Flash Memory Chips

2. Zero Out Technique

FORUM 18

Data Protection

Article Overview

There is considerable evidence that industry, government and education hold insufficient protection against data losses. It may be that managers are not fully aware of the information security risks and the best available investments in technology to control databases, hardware and software. How can we as a nation better meet the ethics of responsibility?

Article: *93,754,333 Examples of Data Nonchalance*

By TOM ZELLER, JR.
September 25, 2006
LINK BY LINK

Less than two years into the great cultural awakening to the vulnerability of personal data, companies and institutions of every shape and size — like the data broker ChoicePoint, the credit card processor CardSystems Solutions, media companies like Time Warner and dozens of colleges and universities across the land — have collectively fumbled 93,754,333 private records. Or at least that's the rough figure the Privacy Rights Clearinghouse, a consumer advocacy organization in San Diego, has tallied thus far.

An entry from Sept. 7: Chase Card Services, a division of J. P. Morgan Chase, announced that it had begun notifying 2.6 million current and former Circuit City credit card account holders that computer tapes containing their personal information had been inadvertently tossed in the trash.

The bank said it believed the tapes were safely "buried in a landfill" somewhere, but it was nonetheless offering affected consumers the now pro forma consolation prize: one year of free credit monitoring.

Last Thursday, another entry was logged. The Commerce Department announced that between 2001 and the present, 1,137 laptops — or about 4 percent of its total inventory — were lost, missing or had been stolen from its 15 operating units. The largest number, 672, had been in use at the Census Bureau, the department reported, and 246 of those contained "some degree of personal data," although it maintained that a combination of passwords and "complex data formats," among other things, would limit the risk that the information could be misused.

"While we know of no instance of personal information being improperly used, we regret each instance of lost material," Commerce Secretary Carlos M. Gutierrez said in a statement, "and believe the volume of lost equipment is unacceptable."

Taking a wider view of things, though, one might say the volume of lost consumer data remains almost comically epidemic. Hackers and sophisticated data thieves are one thing. But in the battle to stop the great hemorrhaging of personal data, the enemy is us.

It was only four months ago, after all, that the United States Department of Veterans Affairs was forced to announce that a laptop and external hard drive containing personal information, including names, Social Security numbers, and dates of birth on roughly 28 million veterans — just shy of 10 percent of the entire United States population — had been stolen from an agency employee's home.

The equipment was recovered in late June, and in August, two teenagers were arrested in connection with the theft. The F.B.I. has indicated that the data appears to have not been accessed, but practices at the veterans department — where so much sensitive information on so many Americans was being ported to a suburban living room for weekend work — were a study in data nonchalance.

And of course, it's not just a government problem.

Incidents run the gamut: In early June it was revealed that the names, addresses and credit and debit card numbers of some 243,000 customers of Hotels.com were lost to the wind when a laptop holding the data was spirited away by a thief. The device, which belonged to an employee of Ernst & Young, the auditor for Hotels.com, had been left in a locked car. (Well, locking the car was smart, right?)

The names and Social Security numbers — and in some instances medical histories — of some 51,000 current and former patients of PSA HealthCare, a major provider of pediatric home care services for children, were on a laptop stolen from an employee's car on July 15. Computer tape with information on nearly 10,000 employees of the California Department of Mental Health has also apparently gone missing. (The employees were notified by e-mail Aug. 17). And 612 Aflac insurance policy holders were notified on Aug. 11 that a laptop containing their names, addresses, Social Security numbers and dates of birth was pilfered, yet again from an agent's car. (Readers can visit the Privacy Rights scoreboard at privacyrights.org/ar/ChronDataBreaches.htm for more sobering tidbits.)

But a survey of 484 United States-based information technology departments within business or governmental organizations, published in August by the Ponemon Institute, a privacy consulting company, and sponsored by the data security firm Vontu, tells the real story here.

The survey found, among other things, that more than half of corporate laptops contained unprotected sensitive data, that one in 10 laptops is stolen and that 97 percent of those are never recovered. The study also found that 81 percent of firms reported that an "electronic storage device such as a laptop" specifically containing sensitive or confidential information had been lost or stolen in the past year.

If nothing else, the Commerce Department can be comforted by the fact that its loss of 1,137 laptops over the last five years is hardly unusual.

But the problem is real, said Joseph Ansanelli, the chief executive and founder of Vontu, who has testified before Congress on privacy problems. And it isn't going to be solved by relegating security entirely to passwords and encryption — although that is necessary.

Just as important, Mr. Ansanelli suggested, is simply paying attention, from a policy perspective, to who has access to what data, why, how it's being moved, where it's being moved to — and establishing clear rules to govern it all.

"Only by focusing on understanding where data is stored and where it is going can organizations better protect information and prevent it from being carried or sent insecurely," Mr. Ansanelli said. "Taller fences or more locks on the doors won't help."

And if institutions entrusted to handle personal information don't start getting serious about their stewardship, they may have their hand forced.

"The costs are high to losing customer data, intellectual property or even worse, national intelligence data," Mr. Ansanelli said. "And if organizations do not stop the insanity of data loss, Congress will be forced to act and mandate new protections for all this information."

O.K., just one more: On Aug. 9, the inspector general's office at the United States Department of Transportation reported that a laptop belonging to a special agent working out of Miami was stolen from a government-owned vehicle on July 27 in Doral, Fla. It contained the names, addresses, Social Security numbers and dates of birth — an identity thief's toolkit, in other words — on more than 132,000 individuals.

Things to Think About

1. What is the "pro forma consolation prize"? Is it sufficient? Explain.

2. What is data nonchalance? Does it exist in your personal life? Have you seen evidence of this at an organization for which you have been employed either part-time or full-time?

3. The author makes the case that the problem is not hackers and sophisticated data thieves. What is the problem? Who is the problem?

4. Should the U.S. Department of Veterans Affairs allow an employee to take a laptop with classified information home? When more than half of corporate laptops contain unprotected sensitive data, one in ten are stolen, and 97% of those are never recovered, what kinds of policies should be implemented?

5. Why might laptops be a greater concern than desktops?

Key Terms

1. Intellectual property

2. Identity thief's toolkit

FORUM 19

Wireless Computing

Article Overview

The WiMax (Worldwide Interoperability for Microwave Access) is wireless broadband access technology that is considered the next revolution in wireless computing. A single hotspot (wireless network) delivers up to 40 megabits per second per channel as opposed to a current speed of 1.5 to 3 Mbps. It can deliver enough bandwidth (data speed) to support hundreds of businesses with T-1 speed connectivity. That is roughly 60 times more data than a normal residential broadband speed! Will Intel's World Ahead Program close the digital divide by providing an infrastructure to support this new technology?

Article: *Intel installs wireless 'WiMax' Internet in Amazon island city*

By ALAN CLENDENNING
September 20, 2006 11:19 AM ET
The Associated Press

Intel has created a WiMax network for and donated computers to the 114,000 residents of Parintins, Brazil. A boat transporting 60 desktop computers for computer labs at two schools pulls into the island city's port.

SAO PAULO, Brazil — Intel chairman Craig Barrett traveled to an isolated Amazon River island city on Wednesday to launch wireless Internet access with the company's WiMAX technology, using a satellite link to beam bandwidth to a place where even electricity is hard to come by.

Intel's World Ahead Program, which promotes the use of computers in public areas in developing countries, bankrolled the installation of a WiMAX tower and five spots in the city of Parintins where students, teachers and doctors will now have fast Internet connections for the first time.

Parintins, about 1,600 miles north of Brazil's industrial and financial hub of Sao Paulo, is home to more 114,000 people but has no roads linking it to other cities, so the only way to get there is by boat or airplane.

Like many places around Latin America's largest country, Internet connections are limited to spotty and expensive dial-up links often worse than what most Americans had in the mid-1990s when the Internet started to take off in the United States.

One of the biggest challenges in Parintins for the Santa Clara, Calif.-based chipmaker was a lack of electrical power at the schools, a hurdle Intel overcame by working with the local government.

"I think we're trying to show if you can do it in a remote city like Parintins then you can do it just about anywhere," Barrett said in a telephone interview before heading to Brazil.

WiMAX delivers wireless access over long distances and is suited for remote places that don't have an established infrastructure of power lines or telephone poles.

Intel also is eying spots in the Middle East and Africa to set up WiMAX infrastructure, Barrett said.

"You can bring this capability to anywhere on the face of the earth," he said.

Intel officials declined to specify the investment for getting WiMAX up and running in Parintins, but a team of 50 people spent two months planning and setting up the network and training people to use it. The 330-foot high tower, flown and shipped to Parintins, can supply Internet access in a 31-mile range.

Overall, Intel will spend $1 billion over the next five years with its World Ahead Program, which was started earlier this year and aims to help close the digital divide between developed and developing nations.

Though the Parintins project doesn't provide free Internet throughout the city, Intel said local or state officials could do that relatively easily if they can come up with the money because the tower was the biggest technological hurdle.

For now, two public schools, a hospital, a community center and the city's university have easy Internet access via antennas fed by the tower.

Sixty computers were provided to the schools and the university, and the Parintins doctors were given cameras and other equipment that will allow them to use "telemedicine" to consult about difficult medical conditions with specialists in faraway cities like Sao Paulo.

Parintins Mayor Frank Bi Garcia said the project "will prepare this generation for the future" by helping to reduce the city's isolation from the rest of the world.

Things to Think About

1. How does Intel's program work to close the digital divide worldwide?

2. How does Intel provide bandwidth to remote areas of the world?

3. How does this technology benefit the people of Parintins in terms of quality of life, social links, political links and economic links?

4. What were the challenges faced by Intel, technical, political, etc.?

5. What challenges will now exist for the people of Parintins?

Key Words

1. WiMax Infrastructure

2. Telemedicine

FORUM 20

Technology Infrastructure

Article Overview

Technology infrastructure is at debate. Is the cost of a particular technology worth the return on the investment to the organization? Is it fiscally responsible for an organization to upgrade to more current technology even when the value to the organization does not appear to support the cost? In New York City, where space is at a premium, the law of supply and demand suggests that landlords may not benefit from making the investment. Where does this leave the tenant?

Article: *SQUARE FEET; Wi-Fi for the Building? Depends on the Landlord*

By ALISON GREGOR
August 2, 2006
The New York Times Company

When the technology firm BlueSwitch needed new offices last year, it sought space offering wireless Internet access to minimize downtime during the relocation.

BlueSwitch, a 20-person company that specializes in Web sites and Web-based software, needed to provide services to clients continuously when relocating from its previous office in Downtown Manhattan, so the firm took about 3,000 feet at 61 Broadway, at Exchange Place. Broad Street Development, the landlord, has been retrofitting the entire 653,000-square-foot office building for wireless Internet at the request of tenants.

"We really had zero downtime," said Alex Paskie, a co-owner and director of BlueSwitch. "We were able to access the Internet immediately, and even though we didn't have furniture or soda to drink, we did have connectivity. For us, that's the most important thing."

Other companies, however, may have more difficulty than BlueSwitch in finding wireless Internet access, particularly in Manhattan. Even in a business world where executives are increasingly mobile and working on laptops, most landlords say they have not experienced strong enough demand to warrant their investing in a system to provide wireless Internet in their buildings.

Most tenants are satisfied with offices hard-wired with broadband Internet access, landlords say.

"We have reviewed Wi-Fi, or wireless fidelity, a number of times," said Robert Kantor, president of Time Equities, which has office properties around the country. "Our experience has been that Wi-Fi is used by people who are transient users, and even in our own office, where we thought about putting it in, there doesn't seem to be a need."

The Rockefeller Group, another nationwide owner of commercial space, announced in 2003, when the technology was relatively new, that it would install wireless Internet access in five of its office buildings. The company has since backed off.

"None of our tenants were really demanding it at the time," said Brian Mahoney, a company spokesman.

The Rockefeller Group does have Wi-Fi, however, in the sunken plaza of the McGraw-Hill Building at 1221 Avenue of the Americas. Some landlords have chosen to offer the service in lobbies or plazas to attract users to the spaces, said Stephen D. Heyman, president of Realinsight, which does project management for company relocations, including coordination of information technology services. "If you've got a plaza area, it's a nice amenity to have," Mr. Heyman said.

Some huge mixed-use complexes built by commercial development companies in recent years have included multimillion-dollar infrastructures providing wireless services, but this service seems aimed primarily at potential buyers of very high-end apartments. The Related Companies, developer of the Time Warner Center at 10 Columbus Circle, which includes the Mandarin Oriental Hotel and luxury condominiums, and Vornado Realty Trust, which built 731 Lexington Avenue, between 58th and 59th Streets, which also includes luxury condominiums, have provided wireless service that goes well beyond Internet access.

These wireless distribution systems, installed by InnerWireless, a company in Richardson, Tex., cost anywhere from 75 cents to $2 a square foot to put in — which could reach into the millions of dollars for a very large development.

The antennas installed as part of such a system can be used with many kinds of wireless communications, like mobile phones and hand-held computing devices, which often lose signals in office buildings, along with two-way radios and public safety devices.

InnerWireless has also provided wireless distribution systems for a dozen large companies in New York City and the surrounding area, though company representatives would not reveal names.

When tenants need nothing more sophisticated than simple Internet access, however, many simply set up their own systems, and this may be dissuading landlords from making the investment, Mr. Heyman said. "I don't think anybody's looking for the landlord to do it," he said.

He said some businesses with frequent visitors or sales agents popping in and out might benefit from the convenience of wireless Internet, but its role as a technological advance might be minimal.

"Over the years, buildings have set themselves up and called themselves 'intelligent buildings,' but you have to separate the whipped cream from the sundae," he said.

Gregg Popkin, a senior managing director at the commercial real estate brokerage CB Richard Ellis, said the current market for office space in Manhattan and some other major cities was so tight — with vacancy rates in the single digits — that landlords had no need to provide an amenity like Wi-Fi.

"Years ago, landlords might have sought to incorporate this type of technology into their building and then sell the service back with a markup," he said.

Nowadays, the landlord might even charge the tenant for use of a building's vertical riser to run the antenna needed to disperse the wireless signal. But typically, the landlord would not want to be involved in providing the service, because he "doesn't want any liability if the system goes down," Mr. Popkin said.

Wireless routers can cost as little as $100, so many businesses install their own. For larger businesses, with 100,000 square feet or more, installing wireless Internet access might be less costly than hard-wiring all work stations, Mr. Popkin said.

Still, Broad Street Development has received so many requests from tenants for Wi-Fi at 61 Broadway — especially smaller tenants ranging from 4,000 to 5,000 square feet — that in the future it plans to outfit all of its office buildings with wireless Internet, including a 296,000-square-foot building at 370 Lexington Avenue.

"It's an investment into the real estate, but what we've found is it sets us apart in terms of appealing to tenants," said Daniel M. Blanco, executive vice president of Broad Street Development.

The company providing the wireless Internet infrastructure at 61 Broadway, which is 33 stories tall, is Advanced Digital Networks, which typically charges $2,500 to $10,000 a building, said Tamer Zakhary, the company's president and chief executive. While operating this system costs landlords nothing, other wireless infrastructures can have annual operating costs of 12 to 15 percent of the installation cost, he said.

Besides Broad Street Development, Advanced Digital Networks has done work for New York City landlords like the Rudin Management Company, and for commercial real estate services companies like GVA Williams, Newmark Knight Frank and Cushman & Wakefield, Mr. Zakhary said.

But, in general, New York City is said to be behind many of the country's other large cities in offering wireless Internet to tenants of office buildings. "New York City is not even close to other cities," Mr. Zakhary said.

Things to Think About

1. Define the meaning of technology infrastructure.

2. Why are landlords avoiding support of a wireless infrastructure? Do their clients "need" wireless, as opposed to "want" it? Explain.

3. How can tenants provide their own wireless distribution system?

4. What are intelligent buildings? What does Heyman mean by a need to separate the "whipped cream from the sundae"? Do you agree?

5. Why does Daniel Blanco intend to make the investment? Do you agree with his strategy?

Key Terms

1. Wireless distribution system

2. Wireless Internet infrastructure

FORUM 21

Computer Warfare

Article Overview

War strikes images of soldiers dressed in camouflage and helmets, in tanks and on ships, with guns and grenades as weaponry, prepared to attack and defend. However, there is a large cadre of soldiers whose weapons are computers, databases and networks, their ammunition is made up of malicious code and their potential for casualties are massive. These soldiers are skilled computer programmers.

Article: *Hackers Attack Via Chinese Web Sites, U.S. Agencies' Networks Are Among Targets*

By BRADLEY GRAHAM
August 25, 2005
The Washington Post; p. A01

Web sites in China are being used heavily to target computer networks in the Defense Department and other U.S. agencies, successfully breaching hundreds of unclassified networks, according to several U.S. officials.

Classified systems have not been compromised, the officials added. But U.S. authorities remain concerned because, as one official said, even seemingly innocuous information, when pulled together from various sources, can yield useful intelligence to an adversary.

"The scope of this thing is surprisingly big," said one of four government officials who spoke separately about the incidents, which stretch back as far as two or three years and have been code-named Titan Rain by U.S. investigators. All officials insisted on anonymity, given the sensitivity of the matter.

Whether the attacks constitute a coordinated Chinese government campaign to penetrate U.S. networks and spy on government databanks has divided U.S. analysts. Some in the Pentagon are said to be convinced of official Chinese involvement; others see the electronic probing as the work of other hackers simply using Chinese networks to disguise the origins of the attacks.

"It's not just the Defense Department but a wide variety of networks that have been hit," including the departments of State, Energy and Homeland Security as well as defense contractors, the official said. "This is an ongoing, organized attempt to siphon off information from our unclassified systems."

Another official, however, cautioned against exaggerating the severity of the intrusions. He said the attacks, while constituting "a large volume," were "not the biggest thing going on out there."

Apart from acknowledging the existence of Titan Rain and providing a sketchy account of its scope, the officials who were interviewed declined to offer further details, citing legal and political considerations and a desire to avoid giving any advantage to the hackers. One official said the FBI has opened an investigation into the incidents. The FBI declined to comment.

One official familiar with the investigation said it has not provided definitive evidence of who is behind the attacks. "Is this an orchestrated campaign by PRC or just a bunch of disconnected hackers? We just can't say at this point," the official said, referring to the People's Republic of China.

With the threat of computer intrusions on the rise generally among Internet users, U.S. government officials have made no secret that their systems, like commercial and household ones, are subject to attack. Because the Pentagon has more computers than any other agency — about 5 million worldwide — it is the most exposed to foreign as well as domestic hackers, the officials said.

Over the past few years, the Defense Department has taken steps to better organize what had been a rather disjointed approach to cyber security by individual branches of the armed forces. Last year, responsibility for managing the Pentagon's computer networks was assigned to the new Joint Task Force for Global Network Operations under the U.S. Strategic Command.

"Like everybody connected to the Internet, we're seeing a huge spike" in outside scanning of Pentagon systems, said Lt. Col. Mike VanPutte, vice director of operations at the task force. "That's really for two reasons. One is, the tools are much simpler today. Anyone can download an attack tool and target any block on the Internet. The second is, the intrusion detection systems in place today," which are more sophisticated and can identify more attacks.

Pentagon figures show that more attempts to scan Defense Department systems come from China, which has 119 million Internet users, than from any other country. VanPutte said this does not mean that China is where all the probes start, only that it is "the last hop" before they reach their targets.

He noted that China is a convenient "steppingstone" for hackers because of the large number of computers there that can be compromised. Also, tracing hackers who use Chinese networks is complicated by the lack of cyber investigation agreements between China and the United States, another task force official said.

The number of attempted intrusions from all sources identified by the Pentagon last year totaled about 79,000, defense officials said, up from about 54,000 in 2003. Of those, hackers succeeded in gaining access to a Defense Department computer in about 1,300 cases. The vast majority of these instances involved what VanPutte called "low risk" computers.

Concern about computer attacks from China comes amid heightened U.S. worry generally about Chinese military activities. Defense Secretary Donald H. Rumsfeld warned in June that China's military spending threatened the security balance in Asia, and the Pentagon's latest annual report on Chinese military power, released last month, described the ongoing modernization of Beijing's armed forces.

The report contained a separate section on development of computer attack systems by China's military. It said the People's Liberation Army (PLA) sees computer network operations as "critical to seize the initiative" in establishing "electromagnetic dominance" early in a conflict to increase effectiveness in battle.

"The PLA has likely established information warfare units to develop viruses to attack enemy computer systems and networks, and tactics to protect friendly computer systems and networks," the report said.

"The PLA has increased the role of CNO [computer network operations] in its military exercises," the report added. "Although initial training efforts focused on increasing the PLA's proficiency in defensive measures, recent exercises have incorporated offensive operations, primarily as first strikes against enemy networks."

The computer attacks from China have given added impetus to Pentagon moves to adopt new detection software programs and improve training of computer security specialists, several officials said.

"It's a constant game of staying one step ahead," one said.

Staff writer Dan Eggen contributed to this report.

Things to Think About

1. What is the job of information warfare units of the PLA?

2. If it has been determined that classified systems have not been compromised by the Chinese, why do you think that U.S. officials are concerned?

3. Describe Operation Titan-Rain. Some U.S. analysts are convinced of official Chinese involvement. What do analysts recognize as the other possibility?

4. Why is China considered a convenient "steppingstone" for hackers? How many computers does the Pentagon have worldwide? How many Internet users are in China?

5. How is the Pentagon responding to these concerns?

Key Terms

1. Operation Titan Rain

2. Information warfare

FORUM 22

Data Recovery

Article Overview

Data loss anxiety, perhaps coupled with the Ethics of Responsibility, compels us to backup our data to the multitude of storage devices available. In the wake of the tragedy of 9/11/01, organizations and individuals are ever more vigilant. Research, however, indicates that most of us lose our data due to an accident or natural disaster. This seems to suggest, that in some instances, we may have little control over loosing our data. What are the consequences of losing data? Is recovery available to assist in recouping data? What are the extraordinary costs?

Article: *PC crashes. Data gone. Deep despair. Couldn't happen to you, right? Wrong*.

By CHRIS TUCKER
American Way Magazine
April 2004

What does Keith Richards, the Rolling Stones' legendary bad boy, have in common with Leslie Contreras, a mild-mannered human resources consultant for Ernst & Young.

Both share, with millions of other computer users, a peculiarly modern condition called Data Loss Anxiety, or datanois — the fear of losing those ever-larger chunks of our lives stored on our PCs.

We'll get to Richards in a moment. For Contreras, datanoia struck while she was out of town one weekend last year. An upstairs neighbor's toilet overflowed and ran for hours before anyone discovered the problem. By that time, water had seeped into Contreras' apartment, dousing her PC. At first, though, it looked like the digital gods had smiled on her. The machine booted up and ran for a day. "Then it died," Contreras recalls. "The screen froze. I couldn't do anything."

Like many other PC users, Contreras had never backed up her system. And like any other PC user, she desperately needed that vast collection of 1's and 0's housed on her comatose machine.

This was more important than any work-related stuff", she says. "I had three years of pictures, favorite music, all the papers I'd written in college, and thousands of e-mails stored on my hard drive."

Thus began a month-long odyssey of frustration, failure, and eventual success.

She called the computer manufacturer's helpline and spent hours following a technician's instructions. Nothing. Then, she took the wounded unit to a big-box electronics store, where she was granted a glimmer of hope: Her desktop appeared, showing all those beautiful icons representing family and friends. But when the technician later moved the unit to another workstation, darkness fell again. Nothing.

Over the next two weeks, Contreras ran through her options. A local PC shop? Sorry. A friend's techish pal? Nope. A company IT guy? Uh-uh. Nearing despair, she mailed the hard drive to a company that specializes in difficult data-recovery jobs, prepared to spend up to $2,000 to regain her info. But a few days later, the company reported failure.

"They even offered to dispose of the hard drive for me, but for whatever reason, I just wasn't ready to kiss it goodbye yet," says Contreras.

So she tried one more gambit, sending her hard drive to a Minnesota-based company named Ontrack Data Recover. She was at work when she received an e-mail from Ontrack. The bad news: A handful of files were hopelessly corrupted. The good news: Thousands of files had been rescued from their digital limbo. The salvage work cost about $1,800, but Contreras considers it money well spent.

"I just wanted to kiss everyone at Ontrack," she says. "They achieved what nobody else thought was possible."

Data Detectives

 It's hard to get exact figures on how much data loss costs America in lost productivity and money. According to one study by Pepperdine University, about six percent of all PCs suffer a missing-data incident each year. Assuming the average cost of each recovery to be around $2,000, the study concludes that a Fortune 1000 company of 50,000 employees, each with one PC, spends $7.6 million yearly on lost PC data.

Ripple that through the economy, add in the vast anecdotal evidence from people like Leslie Contreras, and we're looking at a monumental problem. Officials at privately held Ontrack Data Recovery won't disclose how many rescue jobs they undertake each year, but they claim a success rate of better than 80 percent and say they'll recover at least a petabyte of data in 2004, a number almost beyond imagining. If a single CD-ROM holds 650 megabytes of data, we'd need 1.6 million CD-ROMS to house a petabyte. Let's put them in your office, not mine.

Experts in data loss recovery point to three main causes of our digital disasters: mechanical failure; user error; and viruses, natural disasters, and other weird tricks of fate. To see some of the more bizarre accidents that can befall a computer, check out the "Museum of Disk-asters" on the website of California-based DriveSavers, a leading data-recovery service. There you'll see a laptop that spent two days at the bottom of the Amazon River, an iMac reduced to a twisted pile of slag in a house fire, and other oddities. John Christopher, an engineer at DriveSavers, says the company frequently gets these extreme cases, like the New York City exec whose laptop was crushed by an 18-wheeler. Citing a 90 percent success rate, Christopher says they were able to pull his data out of the wreckage.

DriveSavers has garnered plenty of publicity by helping high-profile celebs and entertainers survive data-loss nightmares. Website testimonials from the likes of Sean Connery, Barbara Mandrell, Sting, and Keith Richards sing the company's praises. Richards lost vital info just prior to a Stones' American tour and turned to DriveSavers for a more-than-emotional rescue. (Yes, we'd all like to know just what Richards spilled on his computer, but Christopher won't tell.)

Ontrack has its own collection of above-and-beyond stories. During the first Gulf War, the company dispatched engineers to Kuwait to recover a damaged computer system that managed the country's border patrol. The company also did remote recovery, via the Internet, for computers in Nagano, Japan, during the 1998 Winter Olympics. Jim Reinert, Ontrack's director of software and services, can curl your hair with tales of PCs stored in dusty pig barns or dropped in soapy bathwater. And then there was the frazzled businessman who put a bullet through his laptop — thankfully, not while it was in his lap.

Who's Got Your Backup?

I'd like to reveal a brand new, absolutely foolproof, effortless, low-carb solution that will ensure you'll never loses another byte of data. Alas, there isn't one. Ask any expert or any data-loss survivor, and they'll tell you the same things most of us know but don't always do: Install anti-virus software. Keep it current. Back up your files. Back up everything. Backup, backup, backup.

 "A lot of people put anti-virus programs on their computers, but they don't update them," says Carey Holzman, author of *The Healthy PC: Preventive Care and Home Remedies for Your Computer.* "Keep in mind that viruses are written every single day. You need to update at least weekly, if not daily."

As for backing up data, that calls for some form of removable media. For files up to two gigabytes, Holzman recommends flash drives that connect to a LPC's USB port. Ranging in price from about $40 to $350 depending on storage size, many of these devices will fit on a keychain; they're ideal for quick backup. Holzman says they're also more reliable than the older zip drives, which are essentially just big floppy drives. For one thing, flash drives are solid state. "That means no moving parts, no friction, no heat, no wear," Holzman says. "They're virtually indestructible.

For larger files, especially those containing photos or music, use CDs or DVDs. And when you've backed up those precious files, take one more step toward conquering datanoia. "Store the backup copies away from your computer site," Holzlman says.

Leslie Contreras, a born-again backup fan, can't stress this enough. "I've now got a backup for my backup," she says. "I keep one set in a fireproof, waterproof box at home, and I keep another set of backups at my office. I've learned my lesson."

Oh, one other thing. If you live in an apartment, don't put your computer directly below the neighbor's bathroom. PC yes, WC no.

To The Rescue

When the data devils strike, dozens of recovery specialists stand ready to help. Here are two of the largest and most respected.

DriveSavers works on the damaged hard drives from PCs and Macs, and all operating systems, and claims a 90 percent success rate. The average recovery price is about $1,000, and you can get a free estimate by phone. Its offices are in Marin County, California. (800) 440-1904, www.driversavers.com.

Ontrack Data Recovery offers a full range of data-recovery services for PCs, laptops, servers, and other storage media. It claims an 80 to 90 percent success rate. "Remote" recovery service is available via the Internet. The average recovery price is about $1,000 and you can get a free estimate by phone or online. Its offices are in Minneapolis, Los Angeles, Washington, D.C., and New York metro areas. Ontrack also makes its own brand of data-recovery software for home and office. (800) 872-2599, www.ontrack.com.

Chris Tucker, a Dallas-based write and editor, writes Business Trends each month for American Way.

Things to Think About

1. Do you or your colleagues suffer from datanoia? Explain.

2. How much does lost data cost Americans in productivity and money?

3. How much data will Ontrack recover in the course of a year?

4. What does the author identify as the three main causes of digital disaster?

5. What does the article suggest as the most foolproof ways to safeguard data? Could you add to this list?

Key Terms

1. Datanoia

2. Petabyte

FORUM 23

Copyright Infringement

Article Overview

The Motion Picture Association of America, along with the Recording Industry Association of America, are forces to be reckoned with. They regularly lobby Congress for support of their efforts to eliminate Internet piracy. The story that follows may be deemed as one of citizen apathy. It concerns an individual who perhaps has not made an appropriate effort to become responsibly informed and concomitantly, uses ignorance to excuse his disobedience of the law. Rather, you may decide that this is a story of a senior citizen who is the innocent victim of exploitation.

Article: *Grandpa Is Sued Over Grandson's Downloads*

Nov 2, 2005 8:42 AM ET
Milwaukee Journal Sentinel (AP)

A 67-year-old man who says he doesn't even like watching movies has been sued by the film industry for copyright infringement after a grandson of his downloaded four movies on their home computer.

The Motion Picture Association of America filed a federal lawsuit Tuesday against Fred Lawrence of Racine, seeking as much as $600,000 in damages for downloading four movies over the Internet file-sharing service iMesh.

The suit was filed after Lawrence refused a March offer to settle the matter by paying $4,000.

"First of all, like I say, I guess I'd have to plead being naive about the whole thing," he said.

"I personally didn't do it, and I wouldn't do it. But I don't think it was anything but an innocent mistake my grandson made."

Lawrence said his grandson, who was then 12, downloaded "The Incredibles," "I, Robot," "The Grudge," and "The Forgotten" in December, without knowing it was illegal to do so.

The Racine man said his grandson downloaded the movies out of curiosity, and deleted the computer files immediately. The family already owned three of the four titles on DVD, he said.

"I can see where they wouldn't want this to happen, but when you get up around $4,000 ... I don't have that kind of money," Lawrence said. "I never was and never will be a wealthy person."

Kori Bernards, vice president of corporate communications for MPAA, said the movie industry wants people to understand the consequences of Internet piracy. She said the problem is the movies that were downloaded were then available to thousands of other users on the iMesh network.

"Basically what you are doing when you use peer-to-peer software is you are offering someone else's product that they own to thousands of other people for free, and it's not fair," Bernards said. Illegal downloading costs the movie industry an estimated $5.4 billion a year, she said.

Things to Think About

1. Why is peer-to-peer software, such as iMesh, often considered a recipe for disaster among the computer illiterate? Do you agree with Bernards's description of the crux of the problem?

2. What are the consequences of Internet piracy?

3. How could Lawrence have avoided the problem created by his grandson?

4. How much does illegal downloading cost the movie industry?

5. Does naiveté relinquish the end user's responsibility to abide by the law? Argue that Lawrence's actions may be regarded as the antithesis of behavior expected among those who live and govern in a democratic society.

Key Terms

1. Peer-to-peer software

2. MPAA

FORUM 24

Managing Information Systems: Adhocracy

Article Overview

Management in the information systems arena, especially within a decentralized institution of higher education, is often marred by ineffectual strategy, unrealistic budgeting and poor communication. Thomas Kurtz, the co-developer of the BASIC computer language at Dartmouth in 1964, asked, "How can managers make effective decisions about computing and its uses, if they are essentially ignorant of it?" The implication still has meaning for management today. IT managers often report to higher level ranks that lack an understanding of the job requirements of IT personnel as well as the resources necessary to maintain technology systems. With perpetually low investment and general mistrust, costly, yet preventable, errors are inevitable.

Article: *More Holes Than a Pound of Swiss Cheese*
Computer-protection problems at Ohio U. spark complaints from alumni — and firings

By PAULA WASLEY
September 29, 2006
The Chronicle of Higher Education

Linda Couture had been careful to protect herself from identity theft. She avoided both online shopping and banking. She made it a policy never to give out her Social Security number.

So it came as a shock when her alma mater, Ohio University, notified her in May that the data she strove to protect had been compromised in a vast computer-security breach. What made it worse, she says, is that the university did not have a good reason to keep her Social Security number on file some 40 years after she had graduated. And, given the publicity surrounding breaches at several other colleges, she found the university's failure to safeguard her information wholly irresponsible.

Ms. Couture, a retired aerospace executive, says she owes much of her career success to her Ohio University education and until now she had regularly contributed money to the institution. She had intended to leave a sizable gift to the university in her will — something in the five figures — but no longer. "All my good feelings have disappeared," she says.

Ms. Couture is among the thousands of people whose personal information was jeopardized by an unprecedented series of computer-security breaches at Ohio University that left 367,000 files on students, staff, and alumni exposed to hackers over a 13-month period. Five electronic break-ins have angered and alarmed alumni and students, cost the university millions of dollars, and led to the firing of two IT administrators and the resignation of a third. Although many colleges have had breaches, Ohio's are perhaps the most extensive.

Moreover, the electronic break-ins could have, and should have, been avoided, observers say, arguing that officials at Ohio ignored many warning signs.

The troubles at Ohio University are also proof that network breaches can have serious and far-reaching consequences. On the legal front, the university is now facing a potential class-action lawsuit by people whose data were lost. But the institution has also suffered damage to its reputation and its relationships with alumni — as evidenced by a two-foot stack of angry letters from former students, now sitting in the university's legal-affairs office.

An e-mail message sent by the vice chairman of Ohio's Board of Trustees, C. Daniel DeLawder, to the board's secretary soon after the breaches were announced captured the frustration of both administrators and alumni: "When I see one error that was preventable, I attribute it to lax execution on the part of an individual, or perhaps a weak control point," wrote Mr. DeLawder. "When I see three incidents in three distinct areas of an organization the size of Ohio University, I fear we have more holes than a pound of Swiss cheese."

Long Undetected

In late April, an FBI agent showed up at Ohio University with computer hard drives in hand. In the course of other investigations, agents had discovered a duplicate of files from the university's business-incubator center, indicating that a server at the center had been hacked.

At first the university's chief information officer and associate provost for information technology, William F. Sams, was not worried. "We thought there was no sensitive data on that server, except perhaps some technological patent info," he says.

It wasn't until a few days later that someone remembered that the server also contained 35 Social Security numbers attached to parking passes.

By that time, someone outside the university had notified university officials that Ohio University servers were attacking his Web site, prompting the institution to run a diagnostic scan of its network. That scan turned up something far more alarming: An IT security team discovered that a server for the university's alumni-relations office had been hacked some 13 months earlier, in March 2005. The server, which computing officials believed was offline, had been left connected to the network, where hackers had discovered it and used it as a music file-sharing server.

As a result, 300,000 files containing personal information about alumni and university staff members, including 137,000 Social Security numbers, had been exposed for more than a year.

Subsequent searches by university officials revealed yet more break-ins that had gone undetected:

- a computer that housed tax forms for 2,480 vendors and university contractors had been breached since at least August 2005.

- a computer used for online business transactions that contained fragments of personal information including some Social Security numbers and 12 credit-card numbers had been left open to intruders.

- far worse, a server at the university's health center had been broken into in December 2005, leaving the medical records of thousands of current and former students, professors, and staff members exposed for five months.

In early May, Ohio had sent out e-mail messages to the hundreds of thousands of alumni affected by the alumni-office breach. But 10 days later, the university had to send out another 60,000 letters, many to the same individuals, to inform them that information such as dates of birth, Social Security numbers, and medical conditions had also been compromised.

Consultant Called In

The university believes that the five breaches, which are still under investigation by the FBI and local police, are unconnected, and that the data, although exposed, have not been accessed and therefore have not been used to steal individuals' identities.

The university also says it took quick action once it discovered the break-ins. Within three weeks the university spent $750,000 on an emergency effort to shore up the security of its core servers. It also brought in an outside consultant to determine what had gone wrong.

In its audit, Moran Technology Consulting, of Naperville, Ill., concluded that the university had made technology security a "perpetually low priority investment." Chronic underfinancing, poor training, and inadequate staffing, the firm said, had created a "quasi combative" silo culture within central IT administration in which two departments, communication-network services and computer services, operated autonomously with minimal cooperation or communication. The result was a "virtual absence of strategies, policies, designs, and plans to secure the university and its confidential data."

The Moran group's 55-page report laid particular blame for the breaches on two system administrators, Thomas Reid, the director of communication network services, and Todd Acheson, the Internet and systems manager. In particular, the report criticized Mr. Reid for operating with an annual departmental surplus of $1.38-million and spending money on employee health-club memberships while failing to invest in a perimeter fire wall for the university's network. (Mr. Reid contests many of the findings of the Moran report, including its statements about the budget surplus, which, he says, was part of a capital accrual account set aside by the university to replace an aging telephone switch.)

In response, the university's Board of Trustees hastily voted to pump $4-million into patching up the network's security problems and restructuring the university's computer services from the ground up. Based on the findings of the Moran report, Mr. Reid and Mr. Acheson were suspended and eventually fired, while Mr. Sams declared his intention to step aside as CIO. "It has become clear to me that a new energy level and skill set is going to be required in order to allow our IT organization to realize its potential," he announced in a written statement.

Unheeded Warnings

The audit's conclusions, and the lapses that prompted them, should have been no surprise to anyone, say those familiar with the university's computer system.

"Ohio University's IT security vulnerabilities have been known for decades," wrote Douglas Mann, an assistant professor at Ohio who preceded Mr. Sams as associate provost for information technology, in a June 1 memo critiquing the Moran report.

In 2004 the then-provost, Stephen Kopp, expressed concern to *The Chronicle* over the university's severely disorganized computer services, which had grown through the "spontaneous mushrooming of IT people on campus" rather than as the result of a well-defined systematic plan. During his tenure several internal and external studies pointed out the same problems later identified by the Moran group. A 2004 report by outside consultants, the Boulder Management Group, describes the university's IT departments as an "adhocracy" characterized by poor communication and "general mistrust" among administrators, duplicated tasks and resources, and a "lack of unified strategic decision making."

Mr. Reid, who was fired this summer in the wake of the security revelations, says that since 1998 he had repeatedly warned superiors about security risks relating to the proliferation of university servers but that his requests for additional financing and staff went largely unmet. He is appealing his dismissal before a university grievance board and has filed a lawsuit against the university to release records relating to his case. He points out that the university had cut the IT budget by $1-million since 2004, including a 3-percent reduction in 2005 and a 12-percent reduction in 2006. The strains placed on his department by these budget cuts were exacerbated, he says, by an unclear IT command structure and the frequent turnover at the CIO level. "I've had 13 bosses in 22 years," he says.

'I Tried to Warn Them'

The breaches were certainly no shock to Jeremy Valeda. Four years ago, while he was a junior at the university majoring in computer science, Mr. Valeda stumbled upon evidence of the university's lax security while he was testing an online voting system for the student government. He says he discovered that he could easily access sensitive files containing students' Social Security numbers, transcript and degree information, and library fines — and that anyone could change some of the data.

He presented his findings to the Student Senate. "I tried to warn them about it," he says. "I was trying to say, if I can do this, what are the odds that other people can do this?" Mr. Valeda was promptly removed from his voluntary position in the student government, and suddenly faced disciplinary hearings, possible expulsion from the university, and, as an international student from the Philippines, potential deportation for hacking the university's system. Eventually, he says, administrators dropped the case against him. But, to his surprise, no one ever approached him about his findings or seemed to take any action to determine the scope of the vulnerabilities. "Had nothing happened in the future, I would say that would have been a fine course of action," he says. "But since the student information was hacked, it's very embarrassing now."

Mr. Valeda was one of the thousands of alumni to receive a letter in April notifying him that his personal data had been compromised. It now hangs on the wall of his New York apartment, right next to a framed 2003 newspaper clipping, "Student Hacks; Accesses System."

Outpouring of Outrage

Mr. Valeda's reaction was more good-natured than most. In the months since the breaches were announced, more than 8,000 calls and some 800 letters and e-mail messages have flooded in to the university from alumni — most concerned, many angry. The letters, copies of which were made available to *The Chronicle,* contain outpourings of outrage, anxiety, and litigious intent.

"I'm trying to fathom a situation in which a serious breach of Social Security numbers could occur and not be discovered for 13 months," wrote one incensed alumnus. "How could this possibly happen without utter rank incompetence and a carefree attitude toward data security?"

"At the moment, I cringe every time I see my OU sticker on the car because it reminds me of danger," said another. "I am not proud to be a graduate."

As an athletics booster for the university, Robert Moorehead says he and his wife, both Ohio graduates, have always been enthusiastic supporters of the university, especially now that their son is a student there. But with the family hit "from all directions" by the breaches at the alumni and health centers, "that support has been eroded," he says. "Because of my personal relationship to the school and my outspoken public promotion of Ohio University in the past," he wrote in an e-mail message to the university's president, Roderick J. McDavis, "I am ashamed that Ohio University put itself in the position of being the poster child for lax data security."

Like Ms. Couture, numerous alumni hinted or stated outright in letters to the alumni office that they would withhold financial support from the university. Several demanded that the university cover the costs associated with subscribing to credit-monitoring services, including Donald J. Kulpa and Kenneth D. Neben, who in June filed a class-action lawsuit against the university for damages arising from the data theft. One indignant alumnus simply sent the university a bill for $495, an invoice, she explained, for the hours she spent checking her credit. (Ohio declined to pay.)

To date the university has received notifications of identity theft from 33 alumni. But Mr. Sams says that it is nearly impossible to prove that the cases are linked to the Ohio University breaches. In a handful of instances, he says, the fraud occurred before the reported breaches. Although servers were compromised, Mr. Sams says it is likely that hackers did not attempt to access the personal data they contained.

It is too early, say university officials, to determine how severely the breaches will strain the university's relations with its alumni. Many already seem appeased by the frequent public contrition for the breaches by the university's president and the bloodletting in the IT department.

Out of concern for the inflamed sensibilities of alumni, the university has toned down its usual fund-raising efforts this year, eliminating some 3,000 telephone calls and a half-dozen mailings. Alumni officials note that although the university has seen a drop in the number of donations — 3,426 in May and June of this year compared with 4,877 in the same period in 2005 — it has also recorded a sizable increase in the amount donated, from $1.7-million last year to $3-million this year. "A lot of alumni have been very understanding once we've explained the situation to them," says Howard R. Lipman, vice president for university advancement.

Not Alone

However ill-prepared Ohio may have been to face IT security challenges, the university is hardly alone.

In the past two years the nonprofit Privacy Rights Clearinghouse has identified more than 80 data-theft incidents at colleges and universities — many far better financed than Ohio — resulting in the exposure of records containing Social Security numbers, personal account information, and driver's-license numbers. Ohio University holds the record in higher education for sheer number of files that were compromised, but not far behind are the University of Southern California, whose applications database containing files on 270,000 people was hacked in July 2005, and the University of Texas at Austin, where an electronic break-in at the business school in April exposed 197,000 files containing biographical information on students, alumni, and staff members.

The decentralized organizational structures at colleges make them particularly difficult to secure, says Rodney J. Petersen, a policy analyst at Educause, a higher-education technology organization. Unlike corporations, which usually keep data under a single source of control, colleges typically store and use personal information at a departmental level, with servers across campus managing data as disparate as student meal plans, library databases, academic research, and performing-arts-center ticket sales.

The challenge for college system administrators, says Mr. Petersen, is to develop security policies that protect the institution's data but are flexible enough to accommodate its varied missions.

Mr. Petersen hopes that the much-publicized fallout from the Ohio University breaches will serve as a valuable lesson for universities on the importance of continuing risk assessment and drive home to administrators that security lapses' "negative impact on reputation and potential legal liability far outweigh the cost of dealing with issues proactively."

In July, Ohio University announced a 20-point "blueprint" for increasing IT security that includes many of the measures — such as classifying data by the level of security required, reducing the use of Social Security numbers within university databases, and reorganizing computer services with a clear chain of command and responsibility — that Educause recommends as standard practice.

"Hopefully," says Mr. Petersen, "other institutions can learn from their experience and not wait to develop plans to put into practice after the fact."

SECURITY BREACHES AND THEIR AFTERMATH

April 2: Federal Bureau of Investigation contacts Ohio U.'s Innovation Center to advise officials that the center's server — containing e-mail messages, patent and intellectual-property files, and 35 Social Security numbers — has been compromised.

April 24: An alumni server breach is discovered, 13 months after an electronic break-in that exposed Social Security numbers of 137,000 individuals.

May 4: A major security break-in is discovered at the computer system of the university's Hudson Health Center. The system contains personal information, including the dates of birth, Social Security numbers, and clinical information for 60,000 current and former students, professors, and staff members.

May 23: A forensic scan detects that a computer server housing Internal Revenue Service 1099 forms for 2,480 vendors and independent contractors has been hacked, as has a computer used for online business trans-actions that contains personal information including Social Security numbers and 12 credit-card numbers.

June 22: Ohio U. releases a report by Moran Technology Consulting, which had been hired to investigate the breaches, that says the university has made information technology a "perpetually low priority."

June 23: The university's Board of Trustees approves spending $4-million to bolster IT security.

July 10: William F. Sams, Ohio U.'s chief information officer, announces his resignation.

July 28: The university unveils a 20-point "blueprint for building a world-class IT function at Ohio U."

August 3: Thomas Reid, director of communication-network services, and Todd Acheson, manager of Internet and systems, are fired for failing to protect the computer system. (Both men have challenged that decision.)

AT OHIO U.: BIG PROBLEMS, BIG CONSEQUENCES

The Damage:

5 separate systems breached

173,000 Social Security numbers compromised

367,000 personal files exposed, some for more than 13 months

33 reports by alumni about possible identity theft as a result of the breaches

The Reaction:

8,000 calls to an information hotline set up to field concerns

800 e-mail messages and letters of complaint received

34,000 hits on Ohio U.'s data- security Web site

The Cost:

$77,000 spent notifying alumni and students of breaches

$750,000 in 21-day emergency-response expenses for hardware and consulting

$4-million allotted by the Board of Trustees to secure IT systems

2 IT administrators fired

Things to Think About

1. The consultant to Ohio University described general adhocracy in the management of technology at the institution. Explain. What is your opinion?

2. What suggestions for improvement did the consultant make? Would you have included additional suggestions? Explain.

3. Why did the university ignore the many warning signs? Is there an ethical and/or legal dilemma in having fired the individual who warned top officials of the problem? Could the situation be described as a whistle-blower firing? Explain your position.

4. Argue the position that if the university had made an appropriate investment in technology at the outset, they would have saved hundreds of thousands of dollars.

5. How does the decentralized organization of colleges make them particularly difficult to secure? What suggestions were made to overcome this problem?

Key Terms

1. Decentralization

2. Adhocracy

FORUM 25

Online Piracy

Article Overview

Software piracy is a federal offense that imposes fines of up to $150,000 per title infringement. Is it the responsibility of a community of scholars to use its resources to install software barriers to behaviors that may violate the law? Is academic freedom, a protection considered essential to the core of the mission of the academy, at risk when an external organization seeks the support of politicians to invoke measures that enforce the rule of law?

Article: *At Congressional Hearing, Entertainment Officials Say Colleges Do Too Little to Fight Online Piracy*

By BROCK READ
September 27, 2006
The Chronicle of Higher Education

Entertainment-industry officials, often using pointed language, argued at a Congressional hearing on Tuesday that most colleges have not taken sufficient steps to discourage students from downloading pirated music and movie files.

At the hearing, held by a U.S. House of Representatives subcommittee, the officials intensified their attempts to press colleges to offer campuswide subscriptions to legal downloading services, and to install software that can block students from trading copyrighted material on peer-to-peer networks.

About 140 institutions have signed up with such legal services, and more than 60 now use the industry's preferred blocking tool. But many campus administrators — citing, among other factors, concerns about privacy and academic freedom — have been reluctant to restrict network traffic or to encourage students to use a particular online music service.

During several previous hearings, industry representatives had sought to portray colleges as partners in the fight against piracy. But on Tuesday, the heads of the largest music and movie trade groups sharply criticized institutions that have chosen not to adopt antipiracy tactics endorsed by the industry.

"We have heard the reasons for inaction: academic freedom, privacy, 'we're not the music industry's police,'" said Cary H. Sherman, president of the Recording Industry Association of America. "I have no doubt that these are real concerns. But to me, at least, they've begun to sound like excuses."

Mr. Sherman said he was "grateful" to colleges and universities that have used legal downloading services and blocked illegal peer-to-peer transactions, but he argued that "there are a far greater number of schools who do not understand, or simply choose not to acknowledge, their responsibility to help solve the problem."

Daniel R. Glickman, president of the Motion Picture Association of America, seconded Mr. Sherman's criticism of institutions that have not used the entertainment industry's preferred antipiracy tactics. "Some schools have really stepped up to the plate, and some haven't," Mr. Glickman said.

He also asked that college officials be required to provide periodic updates to the panel that held the hearing, the education committee's Subcommittee on 21st Century Competitiveness, on their efforts to curtail campus piracy.

Mr. Sherman and Mr. Glickman stopped short of asking lawmakers to force colleges to subscribe to legal services or block peer-to-peer transactions. But members of the subcommittee raised the specter of federal legislation several times. Rep. Dale E. Kildee of Michigan, the subcommittee's top Democrat, said Congress had considered an amendment that would have stripped federal funds from colleges that did not take antipiracy measures when it debated a bill this year to reauthorize the Higher Education Act (HR 609). The amendment, he said, was ultimately rejected as "too drastic."

William W. Fisher, director of the Berkman Center for Internet & Society at Harvard Law School, agreed with that assessment during his testimony before the subcommittee. Mr. Fisher said software that attempts to block illegitimate file sharing may limit perfectly legal, and academically useful, applications of peer-to-peer networks. "It's not as though they are sitting on their hands," he said of colleges that have shied away from filtering peer-to-peer transactions.

Two university administrators also testified. William E. Kirwan, chancellor of the University System of Maryland, discussed his new role as co-chairman of a committee of college officials and entertainment-industry executives that is examining ways to combat campus piracy. And Cheryl Elzy, dean of libraries at Illinois State University, described her institution's plan to create "a sort of *Consumer Reports* for downloading services."

In the meantime, the recording-industry trade group has sent letters to about 700 American colleges, informing them that the industry would resume its practice of suing college students suspected of music piracy. The trade group will notify colleges when it intends to sue their students, but will let those students settle cases before actually filing the suits, according to industry officials.

"In the next few weeks," the letters say, "we will announce a new university enforcement program that focuses substantially on students who ignore warnings and continue to engage in illegal downloading of music."

Things to Think About

1. Entertainment industry officials accuse college students of trading copyrighted material on peer-to-peer networks. How is this accomplished by students? Why is the peer-to-peer network site not held liable?

2. The entertainment industry officials ask colleges to provide campus-wide subscriptions to legal downloading services. Is it possible that these officials represent those who have a vested financial interest in these services? In other words, could there by a conflict of interest?

3. Why might colleges be reluctant to encourage students to use a particular online music service? What about Fisher's statement?

4. Is it the responsibility of industry officials to assist in providing online music services that utilize advertising as revenue in order to provide services free of charge?

5. Mr. Sherman and Mr. Glickman appear to be seeking a legal response. Congress had considered an amendment that would have stripped federal funds from colleges that did not take antipiracy measures when it debated a bill in 2006. Debate for and against this effort.

Key Words

1. Berkman Center for Internet & Society

2. Peer-to-peer

FORUM 26

Podcasting

Article Overview

The fusing of *broadcasting* and *Ipod*, brings podcasting. Podcasts are pre-recorded audio files that can be posted to text-based blogs in the form of MP3 music files. In addition, the recordings can be retrieved from a computer or downloaded to a handheld device, such as Apple's iPod. The use of iPods in higher education gained media attention in 2004 with the announcement that Duke University would provide each incoming freshman an iPod, preloaded with school information, including a recording of the Duke fight song. Currently, universities are providing podcasts of their class lectures to enhance the classroom experience and provide asynchronous lectures as part of a mobile distance learning program. Are we concerned that for some students, this new use of technology will evolve even further to be used as a substitute for the classroom? Should we be concerned that this will add to the anti-iPod sentiment written about in campus newspapers and promoted on MySpace.com, which even promotes an anti-iPod day?

Article: *Education at hand: Colleges podcast courses to palm-size media players, and students skip that 8 a.m. lecture*

By GADI DECHTER
The Baltimore Sun
September 27, 2006

If they miss this morning's introductory biology lecture, Johns Hopkins University students can still catch it this afternoon — at the lacrosse field, on the light rail, even in bed.

Or wherever they like, whenever they want, provided they have an iPod or some other digital music player.

It's called course "podcasting" — an amalgam of "iPod" and "broadcasting" — and Hopkins is one of dozens of universities making classroom lectures almost instantly available on personal computers and hand-held media players, of which Apple Computer's iPod is the dominant brand.

Some education experts and college officials believe that the trend could alter the college experience, from changing students' study and attendance habits to challenging the basic lecture format itself, something that has largely been fixed since the Middle Ages.

"Learning can now happen anywhere, any time," said Sarita Sanjoy, an instructional technologist at the University of Maryland, Baltimore, which is experimenting with podcasting at several of its professional schools.

There is nothing new about the recording of lectures, a practice that dates at least to the reel-to-reel tape era. And as early as the mid-1990s, colleges and universities were experimenting with letting students hear and watch recorded lectures on university Web sites.

The difference with podcasting is that students are no longer tethered to a computer or to the Internet. They can download individual lectures or "subscribe" to an entire course and have the most recent class automatically added to their iPod or other device.

Once the file is downloaded, it can be heard or watched virtually anywhere. That sounds pretty good to John Ji.

"I'd never go to class at all," the Hopkins neuroscience major said last week, on his way to hear Richard Shingles lecture on the ecological interaction of species. "I'd just sit on the couch and download the podcast and eat potato chips."

The only reason he does show up for general biology — one of a handful being podcast at Hopkins this semester — is because Shingles doles out points for attendance, he said.

Those points are awarded through the use of hand-held voting machines, or "clickers," that students bring to class. Ostensibly designed to facilitate teacher-student interaction in large lectures, the clickers also function as electronic attendance monitors, Shingles acknowledges.

"If it weren't for the [clicker], I would stay at home," Ji said. That attitude makes some professors wary of podcasting altogether.

"It seems this would remove a reason to come to class," said Hopkins philosophy professor Sean Greenberg, who said he would be unlikely to podcast his introductory course on moral philosophy. "I'm not sure we should cater to students' desire to be doing other things during class time."

Such as sleeping in.

Harvard University sophomore Justin Becker said he had no qualms about missing about half of his freshman-year life sciences lectures, knowing he could later watch video recordings of them on a university Web site. Before exams, Becker would review back-to-back lectures at 1 1/2 times their natural speed to maximize cramming efficiency, he said. He got an A.

Though there are as yet no comprehensive studies of the new phenomenon, podcasting advocates say students such as Ji and Becker are the exception. Anecdotal evidence, observers say, shows that most students will still show up in person to downloadable classes.

"The attendance issue is usually the No. 1 thing that people are concerned about, and frankly, it's a huge debate right now," said Obadiah Greenberg, who manages the podcasting program at the University of California at Berkeley.

"Good students will use this to supplement the class. Bad students will use it as a substitute," Greenberg said. "But the fact is that overall, it is a technology that only enhances the classroom experience."

For better or worse, campus-tech trend-watcher Kenneth C. Green believes that podcasting has shown signs of taking root in a way that previous "course-casting" technologies, such as streaming video over the Web, never did.

"It's really taken off in the last year," said Green, director of the Campus Computing Project, a survey of technological trends in higher education begun in 1990. "Podcasting has really taken it to the next plateau."

The key ingredient is familiarity, said Diana Oblinger, a vice president at Educause, a nonprofit association of about 2,000 higher-education information technology professionals.

College students are comfortable downloading music from the Web and transferring it to iPods and other portable devices. And because there's no technical difference between downloading a pop song and downloading a psychology lecture, today's college-age consumers are old hands at the new technology, Oblinger said: "It's a technology that students are familiar with, and they've already got the tools they need to use it."

Perhaps not surprisingly, Apple is a major promoter of the academic podcasting trend, offering free host services to campuses that distribute podcasts through a subsidiary of its iTunes online music store called "iTunes U."

An Apple spokesman declined to say how many campuses have signed up with iTunes U, but so far this year at least 10 have announced their participation, including Berkeley and George Washington University.

At Berkeley, 10,000 people signed up as subscribers and downloaded 250,000 lecture recordings within a week of the school's launch of its iTunes U service in April.

"We have students who are angry with us because we're not podcasting their classes," said Berkeley's Greenberg. "It's really become a high-demand service."

Hopkins, Loyola College and the University of Maryland, Baltimore are also in talks with Apple, according to university officials.

Apple commands about 70 percent of the U.S. digital media player market, according to a recent survey, but students who don't own an iPod, which can cost $80 to $400, can still use iTunes U on most Apple Macintosh or Microsoft Windows-based computers.

It's too early to tell whether lecture podcasts are a just a fad, said Educause's Oblinger.

"I think one of the next steps is going to be for institutions to begin looking at adoption rates: How many people are doing this, how much value do students say they place in it?" she said. "At some point, I'm sure we'll see more scientific studies about whether it makes a difference in someone's learning."

The effect on classroom attendance will also be carefully monitored, though not all universities see less-populated lecture halls as necessarily a negative.

At the University of Maryland, Baltimore, the $142 million dental school building that opened this month was designed with fewer lecture halls because the school anticipates distributing more course content through podcasts and other digital-broadcast technologies, according to restorative dentistry professor Ward Massey, who is also the school's "curriculum innovation coordinator."

While the dental school isn't considering eliminating the lecture format altogether, the number of lectures offered might decrease, Massey said, as the curriculum increasingly includes more so-called hybrid courses where smaller discussion groups are supplemented by virtual lectures that students can download or watch online.

"One option is to have a PowerPoint presentation online and simply put an audio narrative over the top," Massey said. "Or use video clips. All those things could provide an experience that is the same as sitting in a lecture."

That and a bag of chips would be sufficient for Hopkins student Ji.

But even though podcasting hasn't yet saved the 19-year-old junior from the occasional trip away from the couch, he has discovered other advantages to the new technology. For instance, Ji no longer feels any need to take notes in biology or even to crack open the textbook.

When midterms come up this semester, instead of reading the relevant chapters, he'll just listen to the lecture podcasts, following along with the instructors' own notes and slides, which are also provided to students on the course Web site. "Reading," explained Ji, "takes way longer."

Things to Think About

1. The campus newspaper at Ohio University, the *Lantern Edition*, reports that extensive iPod use has created an antisocial, unsafe environment. Students are so distracted that they are no longer cordial, bump into each other in the halls, and risk being hit by cars in the parking lot. With Apple reporting sales of iPods exceeding 8 million in the second quarter of this year alone, one might agree that iPod use has become "fanatical".[1] Will this new use of iPods contribute to the decline of a collegial atmosphere? Explain.

2. Distance learning began as a service to three kinds of students — those who lived in remote locations, those who needed a ubiquitous environment that served their nontraditional, full-time employment schedule, and traditional students — serving to enhance teaching and learning by providing more contact and organization outside of the classroom. Does this article suggest that the use of iPod lectures promotes distance learning among traditional students? What evidence exists? Will this add to the quality of the instruction and the exchange of teaching and learning in the collegial environment? What do you think will be the outcome of the research expected to follow up on this experiment?

3. How do those students who do not have iPods utilize the lectures?

4. In light of Justin Becker's experience and the Dental School plans at University of Maryland, should we expect that the use of iPods for lectures will ultimately lower tuition? Can this be seen as a fiscally responsible move on the part of colleges?

5. Can this technology help students with disabilities and auditory learners?

Key Terms

1. Podcasts

2. Clickers

---

[1] http://www.thelantern.com/media/paper333/sections/20061012Campus.html?norewrite200610121227&sourcedomain=www.thelantern.com

FORUM 27

Wikipedia

Article Overview

When my niece graduated from high school a few years ago, she quickly acted to return the dictionaries she received as gifts from relatives. She was truly astonished. She questioned why anyone would ever use a dictionary when the information could be retrieved so much faster, and the definition provided was so much more comprehensive, when using dictionary.com. Now, perceived as having evolved from the widely trusted electronic dictionary, is a set of encyclopedias which has become the most widely used source of reference information online. While dictionary.com may not concern you, do you regard the integrity of the information provided by Wikipedia as reliable? Can you ensure the credibility of its sources?

Article: *Word Play*

By SAMUEL GREENGARD
American Way Magazine
July 1, 2006

It's one thing to introduce a revolutionary idea. It's an entirely different concept to reinvent the wheel — or in this case, the modern encyclopedia. But Jimmy Wales thinks he has the task covered. Five years ago, the St. Petersburg, Florida, resident advanced the idea of letting the masses write entries to an encyclopedia and then posting all the material online for the world to see. It was bold, it was brash, and it seemingly had no chance to succeed.

Skip forward to 2006, aim your web browser at www.wikipedia.com, and you find out how wrong the pundits were. Wikipedia has grown — "exploded" might be a more apt description — into the world's largest and most widely used source of reference information, with somewhere in the neighborhood of 3.5 million entries and five billion page visits each month. It's free, it's easy to use, and it's more detailed than any other encyclopedia on the planet. There are articles on topics as arcane as navel lint (with links to accompanying photos, no less) and the Huraa Dynasty of the Maldives, and as common as cats and cornflakes.

While every era produces a few standout ideas and products, it's apparent that the 39-year-old Wales — who cut his teeth working as a futures and options trader in Chicago and later introduced a photo search portal that specialized in allowing end users to build "web rings" of content of their own choosing — is rewriting the way people think about and use information. If traditional resources like *Encyclopædia Britannica* and *Columbia Encyclopedia* aim for the scholarly elite, Wikipedia has quite literally emerged as the everyman's encyclopedia.

Consider: Volunteers write every article — and anyone with a web browser and an Internet connection can update them at any time. What's more, it is possible to search the entire Wikipedia database and use the material for any purpose. Already, Wikipedia appears in 123 languages, including Hebrew, Croatian, Tagalog, Vietnamese, and Esperanto. "We're able to harness more brainpower than other encyclopedias," says Wales. "Our approach and format give a distinct advantage over other encyclopedias."

However, not everyone considers Wikipedia a beacon of progress. In recent months, a spate of inaccurate entries have garnered headlines and raised questions about the encyclopedia's integrity. Articles about high-profile and controversial figures, such as President Bush and Sen. John Kerry, have become the target of vandals. Finally, some argue that a highly successful and free Wikipedia could undermine established providers of reference materials and threaten their viability. If these encyclopedias falter, the theory goes, society could wind up with a set of less-than-accurate reference books.

Consider it an irony that the word *encyclopedia* derives from a classical Greek phrase meaning "a general or well-rounded education." Although such reference sets have existed since the sixteenth century — and were once viewed as essential learning and study guides — they have slowly evolved into a source for quick information. Moreover, the advent of CDs, DVDs, broadband, and the web has moved the emphasis away from print and toward pixels. Let's face it: The luster of owning a $1,500 set of encyclopedias isn't what it once was — especially when you consider that they're obsolete as quickly as they are printed.

Wales saw the handwriting on the wall in the late 1990s. The self-professed information freak, who spent countless hours poring over the *World Book Encyclopedia* as a child growing up in Huntsville, Alabama, embarked on a project called Nupedia — a peer-reviewed academic encyclopedia that he now describes as a "complete failure." Although Wales was able to attract "a group of very smart, academic people who were really passionate about the idea, it was too much work for volunteers to deal with," he says.

Rather than toss in the towel, Wales decided to wrap himself around a slightly different approach. Around that time, he was fascinated by wikis — websites that allow users to add and edit content at will (*wiki* is a Hawaiian term that means "quick" or "fast"). Building on the idea of collaborative effort used for Nupedia, why not create a collaborative encyclopedia and tap into the brainpower of the masses? He reasoned that he could harness the same core group that contributed to Nupedia and make content available at no charge — while allowing users to copy and reproduce the encyclopedia at will.

Thus, Wikipedia was born on January 15, 2001. Since then, it has ridden the crest of the Internet wave and emerged as the leading tool for gleaning basic knowledge on almost any given subject. "People are attracted to Wikipedia because it is incredibly easy to use and useful," observes Barry Parr, a media analyst with Jupiter Research. "It's frequently updated, the material can be reproduced freely, and, because of the collaborative way it's written, you get a sense that there are multiple perspectives on any given issue."

What makes Wikipedia remarkable is that you can type in almost any word or subject in the English language and wind up with an article displayed on your computer screen in a fraction of a second. There's no jaunt over to the bookshelf and no shuffling through indexes and cross-references to find a nugget of knowledge. What's more, Wikipedia's million-plus articles in English eclipses Britannica's 80,000, Columbia's 51,000, and Encarta's 63,000. Even more mind-boggling is the fact that Wikipedia adds somewhere around 2,000 entries a day.

Of course, quantity and ease of use don't necessarily equate to quality. Some people, including Joel Waldfogel, Ehrenkranz Professor of Business and Public Policy at the Wharton School of the University of Pennsylvania, question how effectively a spirited cadre of volunteers can produce articles compared to top professionals and luminaries. For instance, Britannica boasts entries from Carl Sagan, Milton Friedman, and numerous Nobel laureates. World Book verifies any fact appearing in any article with at least three respected sources — not including other encyclopedias.

By comparison, Wikipedia is a virtual free-for-all, with more than 13,000 participants churning out articles. If you're inclined to add your two cents' worth, you simply click on a tab at the top of any entry that reads "Edit this page." You make desired changes and click "Save page." Your words are then visible for the entire world to see — though "page patrollers" dutifully track changes (another tab displays the entire history of an article) and verify that the information is appropriate and correct. They also undo vandalized pages — usually within five minutes, Wales says.

Nevertheless, the wiki approach has also led to several faux pas and problems. In 2005, a Wikipedia article linked former newspaper editor and publisher John Seigenthaler Sr. to the assassinations of both John and Robert Kennedy. Seigenthaler, who served as administrative assistant to Attorney General Robert Kennedy, went ballistic. Instead of simply changing the Wikipedia entry — which had appeared from May through October — he penned an editorial for *USA Today* about the "flawed and irresponsible research tool" and his frustration at not being able to identify the anonymous poster. Editors quickly corrected the bio, and a sleuthing book indexer from Texas eventually identified the culprit.

Another high-profile incident occurred last December, when Adam Curry, a former MTV VJ who helped pioneer podcasting, confessed that he had deleted references to rival innovators. That led to charges of "vanity editing." Meanwhile, a summer intern for seven-term Massachusetts Congressman Martin T. Meehan altered his profile to remove an old promise that he would limit his service to four terms. Even Wales has gotten into the act, tweaking his Wikipedia bio at least 18 times — an act that *Wired* magazine referred to as "immature behavior."

Criticism and accusations don't seem to faze Wales. The way he sees it, building Wikipedia doesn't happen overnight — and he is learning on the fly. "We're constantly tweaking and changing to improve the way we manage the process," he says. "While I think the quality of the content is pretty good, I'm cautious about bragging about it, because it's not as good as it should be or will be." In fact, the Seigenthaler incident coincided with changes Wikipedia made to require that new contributors register before submitting articles. It also locked some articles that attract vandalism, yet it still allows open editing by contributors who have editing experience.

Controversy aside, experts insist that Wikipedia is evolving into a reputable source for information. Says Parr: "Wikipedia is climbing into the same league as respected reference guides. It is gaining greater respect every day."

THE BURNING QUESTION IS: Why do so many people volunteer so much time to write and edit entries for Wikipedia? Wales, who spends about 200 days a year crisscrossing the globe to support his passion, says that while contributors' names appear in the "history" section of an article, everlasting glory is the last thing on their minds. "They view this as a charitable and worthwhile mission. They believe that sharing knowledge is beneficial for society," he says. "Many of them also enjoy the social aspects of discussing and debating the finer points of articles and belonging to a community."

David Gerard is a perfect example. The UK-based computer-systems administrator spends upwards of 50 hours per week overseeing pages and handling an assortment of other functions. The self-described trivia fanatic says that Wikipedia offers him a chance to exercise his editing and interpersonal skills. "It's interesting to be able to go into as much depth as you like on a subject without worrying about running out of paper. It feels good to create a useful resource," he says.

Gerard is convinced that Wikipedia's neutral approach resonates with the public. Rather than advocating a single truth or a particular position, Wikipedia articles typically offer a variety of viewpoints, Gerard explains. While absolute neutrality is impossible, and editorial decisions always come down to judgment, "neutral-point-of-view writing on subjects seems to be drastically rare. That's something Wikipedia does that no one else in fact has as a key goal," Gerard says.

The bigger question is how the emerging encyclopedia wars will play out. Some observers, such as Wharton's Waldfogel, believe that Wikipedia has the potential to alter the entire business model for reference materials. "If enough people find that free information is an acceptable substitute for the verified and edited information in traditional encyclopedic sources, they will stop buying and using traditional tools," he says. "The question then becomes: Who is handling the process of gathering and presenting information, and are they producing a reliable product?"

At this point, there's also no proof that Wikipedia can succeed financially. So far, Wales has eschewed advertising and depended solely on contributions to keep the web-based encyclopedia afloat. Last year, the Wikimedia Foundation, which oversees the project, raked in approximately $750,000 in donations (www.wikimediafoundation.org/wiki/fundraising) and pursued grants to help cover costs. Several large companies have also tossed their support behind Wikipedia, including Internet giant Yahoo! Currently, Wikipedia operates with a staff of only three paid employees.

Nevertheless, in addition to Wikipedia, the organization has introduced Wiktionary, the world's largest multilingual dictionary; Wikiquote, a compendium of quotations in more than three dozen languages; Wikibooks, a collection of free, open-content textbooks; and

Wikinews, which features stories based on feeds from news agencies as diverse as ABC Online and Al Jazeera. The latter is part of Wales's ongoing attempt to provide "different perspectives and not wind up as a slave to ratings." Wales also runs a for-profit business called Wikia, which oversees an assortment of online communities supported by ad revenue.

In the end, only one thing is clear: Wales wants the entire world to read and write his book — and so far he is succeeding. In March, Wikipedia ranked as the 18th-most popular site worldwide, ahead of heavyweights like BBC, CNN, and AOL. These days, countless students, journalists, professionals, and others depend on Wikipedia to provide a chunk of knowledge on almost everything. Says Wales: "Wikimedia's mission is to give the world's knowledge to every single person on the planet in their own language. We're on the right path."

Things to Think About

1. How many paid employees are there at Wikipedia? How is the project funded?

2. What other ventures has the organization pursued? Do you believe they will make similar contributions to consumer electronic resources?

3. Why do so many people volunteer so much time to write and edit entries for Wikipedia?

4. Why might the information found on Wikipedia be suspect to researchers? What are the standards for information integrity? What concerns does Ehrenkranz have on this topic? Do you agree?

5. What other criticisms are mentioned? Do you agree?

Key Words

1. Nupedia

2. Wiki

FORUM 28

The Digital Divide

Article Overview

The digital divide has historically addressed the divide that exists between those who have the means to provide personal access to technology, and those who do not, due to the socio-economic factors that separate them. With advances in network technology, a new divide exists based on demographics. This separation affects all socio-economic levels of the populations for which it is problematic — the use of the Internet requires broadband infrastructure for which service providers are not willing to provide rural populations. This time it is about business ROI- the return on investment to providers is not worth the cost. This has severe implications on the economy of rural towns, as businesses cannot compete effectively without access to technology. In a capitalistic economy, is it appropriate for government to intervene or should businesses in the town be forced to close or move elsewhere?

Article: *Rural Areas Left in Slow Lane of High-Speed Data Highway*

By KEN BELSON
The New York Times
September 28, 2006

For most businesses, the goal is to attract as many customers as possible. But in the fast-changing telephone industry, companies are increasingly trying to get rid of many of theirs.

Bill and Ursula Johnson are among the unwanted. These dairy farmers in bucolic northeastern Vermont wake up before dawn not just to milk their cows, but to log on to the Internet, too.

Their dial-up connection is so pokey that the only time they can reliably get onto the Web site of the company that handles their payroll is at 4 in the morning, when it is less busy. Mr. Johnson doubles as state representative for the area, and he doesn't even bother logging on to deal with that. He communicates with colleagues in Montpelier, the capital, by phone and post instead.

The Johnsons' communication agony could soon get worse. Instead of upgrading them to high-speed Internet access, Verizon, their local phone company, is looking to sell the 1.6 million local phone lines it controls in Vermont, New Hampshire and Maine. The possible sale is part of an internal plan called Project Nor'easter, according to a person with knowledge of the details.

A Verizon spokesman, John Bonomo, would not comment on the plan, but said the company "continually evaluates the assets and properties in our portfolio for strategic fit and financial performance."

Verizon is not alone in its desire to reduce the number of landlines it owns. Big phone and cable companies are reluctant to upgrade and expand their networks in sparsely populated places where there are not enough customers to justify the investment. Instead, they are funneling billions of dollars into projects in cities and suburbs where the prospects for a decent return are higher.

But those projects are unlikely to reach rural areas of Vermont and other states, leaving millions of people in the Internet's slow lane, just as high-speed access is becoming more of a necessity than a luxury. The United States already lags behind much of the industrialized world in broadband access.

The lack of broadband has preserved places like Bessie's Diner as Canaan's de facto meeting hall. Over burgers and turkey club sandwiches, local residents swap tidbits that, in a more wired world, might end up in e-mail and instant messages.

Helen Masson, who lost her job at an Ethan Allen furniture factory a few years ago, grumbles that the lack of broadband has made it harder for her to find work, despite taking computer classes. Mr. Johnson, sitting nearby, nods in agreement. "The staff at the statehouse shudder when I'm on a committee because they have to lick a stamp instead of pressing a send button," he said.

Verizon has sold phone lines before. In 2005, the Carlyle Group bought its business in Hawaii. Verizon also sold 1.3 million lines in Alabama, Kentucky and Missouri in 2002.

Others have followed. In May, Sprint Nextel spun off its local phone division with 7.1 million lines and renamed it Embarq. In July, Alltel spun off its local phone group and merged it with Valor Communications.

If Verizon does sell the New England lines, it would most likely be to a smaller company or private equity group that could be even less capable of offering fast Internet access. That prospect has Vermonters fearful that the exodus of jobs and employers from the state could accelerate.

"We have companies that lose money because they don't have broadband," said Maureen Connolly, a director at the Economic Development Council of Northern Vermont. "We're not a third world country. We shouldn't have to beg for service."

While selling off slow-growing landlines in New England may please Verizon's shareholders seeking higher returns, the company's plan has reignited long-simmering political and economic debates about whether the region is being left behind as wealthier states nearby pull further ahead.

The proceeds from any sale of New England lines would help Verizon pay for the potentially more lucrative fiber optic network it is building in and around cities like New York and Boston.

The network is part of Verizon's push to transform itself into a fast-growing technology company and shed its image as a stodgy utility.

The possibility that Verizon would sell local lines is another sign of how much the phone business has changed in the last half decade. Verizon and other former local phone monopolies argue that since the cellphone, cable and Internet companies that are luring away millions of their customers are not compelled to serve remote and rural places, then they should not have to bear that burden either.

In Vermont, Verizon has broadband available on just 56 percent of its 330,000 lines, compared with 95 percent for most local phone companies, which receive substantial federal subsidies. Without the same aid, Verizon must bear more of the financial burden to upgrade its network.

"Vermont — like all rural states — has higher fixed costs of providing service," said Polly Brown, president of Verizon Vermont, where the number of landlines has declined 9.1 percent since 2002. "You're spreading those costs over fewer customers, who are located far and wide, and you're dealing with topographical challenges such as mountains and a rock base."

Residents, unions and politicians in Vermont do not dispute that the phone business is a challenging one, but they say that residents will have a harder time telecommuting or home-schooling their children. Towns like Canaan will not have access to the growing number of government records kept online, they say, and hotels and other tourist attractions will have a harder time attracting outsiders.

Take Michael and Louise Kingston, who have had a summer home in nearby Averill for the last 35 years. Owners of a grape-growing company with vineyards in Chile and California, they often cut their vacations short and return home to New Jersey because they cannot run their business on the 26-kilobit dial-up line — a speed considered fast in 1993 — in Averill.

"It means we can spend less time here, which means you spend less money here at a time when the local economy needs it," Mr. Kingston said.

Connections are so slow that their son drives 25 miles south to Island Pond to find a broadband line. There is no cellphone service either, so when locals go to areas where there is reception, they take along other peoples' phones to retrieve their voice mail for them. In places where Verizon does not sell high-speed Internet, some people have the option of getting broadband from their cable provider. But in Vermont, cable companies have focused on more populous towns like Montpelier and Burlington, the state's largest city. Cable coverage in the northeast part of the state is spotty.

Several rural phone carriers have spoken to Verizon about its lines in New England, including Fairpoint Communications, CenturyTel and Citizens Communications, according to people with knowledge of the discussions. Buyout firms may also be considering the business.

Rural phone lines can be profitable because the basic infrastructure was paid for years ago, there are often few competitors and subsidies from the Universal Service Fund, which helps carriers provide service to hard-to-reach consumers, can be substantial.

But the subsidies do not benefit all carriers equally. For example, Vermont Telecom, which has 21,000 phone lines in the state, will receive $24.34 a month per line in the fourth quarter from the fund, money that is credited to customers on their bills.

But as a larger carrier, Verizon will receive one-tenth the subsidy, or $2.42 per phone line. Any company that buys Verizon's lines will inherit the same subsidies, making such a deal a less attractive investment. Verizon could compensate by lowering its sale price, at the risk of disappointing shareholders.

The economics of providing broadband in rural areas are discouraging, too. The cost of upgrading an existing copper line that runs from switching stations to remote homes can be as much as $5,000, according to the National Exchange Carrier Association. Such costs are prohibitive for phone companies, which typically want to make back their money within three years, said Victor Glass, the director of demand forecasting at the carrier association.

Though frustrations with Verizon run high in places like Canaan, the alternatives are more alarming. Since it took over Verizon's lines in Hawaii, the Carlyle Group has had billing problems that caused a fourfold spike in consumer complaints.

Carlyle's experience could presage what rural areas like northern Vermont might face if Verizon departs, particularly if the buyer sharply cuts costs and jobs.

"We would rather deal with Verizon because there's a process in place and people up and down the food chain that we know," said Darlene Stone, an operator at a Verizon call center in South Burlington and chief steward in the Communications Workers of America, which represents 135 Verizon employees in Vermont. "Private equity funds are not people who are going to be interested in our opinions."

The possibility that a sale could lead to worse service has put regulators in the uneasy position of trying to pressure Verizon to do more while not alienating the company, which invested 37 percent less in its network in Vermont last year than in 2001.

In 2005, the Public Service Board fined Verizon $8.1 million for providing inadequate customer service in Vermont. This year, regulators also got Verizon to agree to expand its broadband coverage to 80 percent of its phone lines by 2010.

That holds out some hope for isolated areas, but there is no guarantee that any particular customer, like the Johnsons, will be among the 80 percent and there is no guarantee that Verizon will still be in Vermont by then.

Alternative broadband providers who could fill that gap face problems, too. Jake Marsh, who runs Island Pond Wireless, a company that beams high-speed Internet signals over strings of antennas, has signed up 250 customers and has a waiting list just as long. But to expand, he is counting on towns getting state funds to help defray the installation costs.

Yet officials in Norton, 15 miles west of Canaan, could not download the 20-page grant application because their dial-up line was so slow.

Things to Think About

1. What is Project Nor'easter? Why are telephone companies trying to get rid of customers? Why does Maureen Connolly compare Vermont with a third-world country?

2. How has the social environment of Vermont been affected? How is the future of education and government jeopardized?

3. How has the loss of broadband negatively affected the economy in New England? What do citizens fear for the future? Why?

4. The author states that Verizon's decisions have to do with image. Could this strategy backfire for Verizon? Explain the Public Service Board fine.

5. Does Verizon have an ethical responsibility to serve these customers? What is Verizon's argument against this?

Key Words

1. Public Service Board

2. National Exchange Carrier Association

FORUM 29

The Software Development Process

Article Overview

A recent trend in government has been to research and implement privatization of services, in order to return a higher quality service at a lower cost. At a state level, for example, some public schools in California, Colorado, Washington, DC, Delaware, Georgia, Iowa, Illinois, Indiana, Maryland, Michigan, Minnesota, Missouri, Nevada, New York, Ohio, Pennsylvania and Wisconsin are run by a private corporation, Edison Schools. Nationally, there is an effort to privatize Social Security, allowing individuals to choose to invest their funds in the stock market. With the development of computer software, however, the opposite scenario appears to hold true. The management of the development of open source software, programs whose code is open to the public and acquired by users at no cost, is superior. Such operations produce higher quality code quicker than commercial outfits. What are the secrets to their success? The National Science Foundation is spending $750,000 to find out.

Article: *Putting Open Source Development Under The Scope*

By JAY LYMAN
October 2, 2006 4:00 AM PT
LinuxInsider

"In a large proprietary software development environment, engineers spend four to nine hours a week in meetings. ... The result of all this is to pace the engineers to the plodding pace of management, so that they can stay in control of the project," said Josh Berkus, core team member of the PostgreSQL open source database project.

Keeping Your Cool in the Datacenter

This white paper discusses today's industry trends and specific needs of a datacenter facing compounding challenges from power and cooling issues. See how Appro's High Performance Servers stack up.

The open source software development process will be going under the microscope as computer science researchers from the University of California Davis use a US$750,000 grant from the National Science Foundation to find out how systems such as the Apache Web server, PostgreSQL database and Python scripting language are built.

Their research will focus on how open source software projects avoid typical departmental or individual slowdowns and manage to produce quality code quicker than commercial, proprietary models.

"The belief in the open source software community is that open access to the source turns on all the available brain power, full blast, on every problem, challenge or opportunity," lead researcher and UC Davis Computer Science Professor Premkuma Devanbu told LinuxInsider. "In traditional products, bits of code tend to be owned or controlled by specific individuals, and thus each bit of code can be on a single-threaded critical path. In open source, anyone can read and comment on a file."

Social Software Study

Successful open source software projects manage to merge social structure and software structure effectively and avoid conventional problems associated with collaborative projects, including pacing by the slowest contributor, Devanbu indicated. Researchers will gain insights into some of these projects by combing message boards, bug reports and e-mail discussions.

"We're not sure yet — we think that there will generally be a convergence of social structure modularity and artifact structure modularity, but it's too early to offer any definite results," Devanbu said. "Prior work by Carliss Baldwin and others comes at it from a different perspective. They argue, using the case of Mozilla, that modularity increases volunteerism. Our goal is to validate these beliefs quantitatively, and it's too early to say for sure." A review of the results is expected within six to eight weeks.

Lesson of Linux

Quality tends to improve with the open source software approach because of modularity, Devanbu noted, which allows a division of labor and knowledge.

"Thus, good design allows implementation to proceed with maximum parallelism and minimum synchronization and coordination," he said.

Poor modularity gives rise to social interaction problems, Devanbu observed, and in turn increases pressure for more modularization, as was the case with Linux.

"As Linux lore has it, when [Linux creator Linus] Torvalds was slow in getting changes to the kernel, the resulting dissatisfaction and flame battles led to the modularization of the kernel and the appointment of lieutenants to oversee each module, which in turn improved the efficiency of the social structure underlying the Linux community of practice," he explained.

It's About the Code

The UC Davis researchers said they would also delve into how open source software projects are able to avoid being paced by the slowest contributors.

One reason may be that open source contributors are brought together by the software itself, as opposed to a job or money, said Josh Berkus, core team member of the PostgreSQL open source database project, which released a beta of its latest version, 8.2, this week.

"It's possible that the software design reciprocally influencing the character of the project participants is something different about open source — mostly because, unlike a company, the code is what holds the community together, not paychecks," Berkus told LinuxInsider.

Secret to Success: No Meetings

How are open source software projects able to set their speed and quality on the best participants? That's simple: "No meetings," Berkus said.

"I'm serious," he continued. "In a large proprietary software development environment, engineers spend four to nine hours a week in meetings, where they are given assignments by managers and expected to work on only their assigned project for the next week. Areas of responsibility are carved out carefully and elaborate quality control and review processes are enforced. The result of all this is to pace the engineers to the plodding pace of management, so that they can stay in control of the project."

Another reason open source development moves more quickly is that engineers are on the projects they want to work on, limiting procrastination and "sandbagging," said Berkus.

Lastly, Berkus explained that open source developers are less apt to work on incorrect or buggy code since the project is their own.

"Open source projects are less likely to follow 'wrong' specifications, because the same people who write the code are the ones setting the goals," he noted.

Things to Think About

1. How is the management of a proprietary software development firm different than a non-profit open source firm? Explain.

2. How will researchers gain insight into how the open source software projects operate? What does this suggest about the tone of your electronic communication when you begin at a job?

3. What does Devanbu suggest about the effects of good design?

4. Explain social structure modularity. How was modularization beneficial in the development of the Linux?

5. What does the author suggest is a common problem of collaborative projects in respect to pace? How does Berkus feel about meetings? What kind of merge is believed to be the backbone of successful open source projects? Do you think that the management lessons learned from this project are well suited for industries other than software development?

Key Words

1. Linux

2. Proprietary software

FORUM 30

Blogger Litigation

Article Overview

Bloggers beware! False statements made over the Internet that damage the reputation of an individual is called libel; for the first time in the 12 years that the Internet has been commercially available, a U.S. blogger lost a libel suit. The precedence that did not exist, now does. The individual found guilty has been ordered to pay his victim $50,000. Worldwide, victims are being recognized by the courts. Professor Chen Tangfa of Nanjing University in China sued Blogcn.com for failing to supervise its online content after the Company refused to delete a post entered by one of his former students. Last summer, Tangfa won. But what did his student write? "Chen Tangfa is indeed an uncouth person. I can see this from his book. He wrote the worst textbook."[1] In the "Wild West of the Internet," will freedom of speech no longer go unchallenged? Does the reaction of the Chinese courts concern us? What are the legal and ethical implications?

Article: *Courts are asked to crack down on bloggers, websites*

By LAURA PARKER
October 2, 2006 10:29 PM ET
USA TODAY

Rafe Banks, a lawyer in Georgia, got involved in a nasty dispute with a client over how to defend him on a drunken-driving charge. The client, David Milum, fired Banks and demanded that the lawyer refund a $3,000 fee. Banks refused.

Milum eventually was acquitted. Ordinarily, that might have been the last Banks ever heard about his former client. But then Milum started a blog.

In May 2004, Banks was stunned to learn that Milum's blog was accusing the lawyer of bribing judges on behalf of drug dealers. At the end of one posting, Milum wrote: "Rafe, don't you wish you had given back my $3,000 retainer?"

Banks, saying the postings were false, sued Milum. And last January, Milum became the first blogger in the USA to lose a libel suit, according to the Media Law Resource Center in New York, which tracks litigation involving bloggers. Milum was ordered to pay Banks $50,000.

---

[1] http://lawprofessors.typepad.com/law_librarian_blog/2006/week31/index.html

The case reflected how blogs — short for web logs, the burgeoning, freewheeling Internet forums that give people the power to instantly disseminate messages worldwide — increasingly are being targeted by those who feel harmed by blog attacks. In the past two years, more than 50 lawsuits stemming from postings on blogs and website message boards have been filed across the nation. The suits have spawned a debate over how the "blogosphere" and its revolutionary impact on speech and publishing might change libel law.

Legal analysts say the lawsuits are challenging a mind-set that has long surrounded blogging: that most bloggers essentially are "judgment-proof" because they — unlike traditional media such as newspapers, magazines and television outlets — often are ordinary citizens who don't have a lot of money. Recent lawsuits by Banks and others who say they have had their reputations harmed or their privacy violated have been aimed not just at cash awards but also at silencing their critics.

"Bloggers didn't think they could be subject to libel," says Eric Robinson, a Media Law Resource Center attorney. "You take what is on your mind, type it and post it."

The legal battles over blogging and message board postings are unfolding on several fronts:

- In Washington, D.C., former U.S. Senate aide Jessica Cutler was sued for invasion of privacy by Robert Steinbuch, also a former Senate aide, after Cutler posted a blog in 2004 describing their sexual escapades. The blog, titled *Washingtonienne*, was viewed widely after it was cited by a Washington gossip website called Wonkette. In July, Steinbuch added Wonkette to the lawsuit.

- Todd Hollis, a criminal defense lawyer in Pittsburgh, has filed a libel suit against a website called DontDateHimGirl.com, which includes message boards in which women gossip about men they supposedly dated. One posting on the site accused Hollis of having herpes. Another said he had infected a woman he once dated with a sexually transmitted disease. Yet another said he was gay. Hollis, 38, who says the accusations are false, is suing the site's operator, Tasha Joseph, and the posters of the messages.

- Anna Draker, a high school assistant principal in San Antonio, filed a defamation and negligence lawsuit against two students and their parents after a hoax page bearing her name, photo and several lewd comments and graphics appeared on MySpace.com, the popular social networking website.

The suit alleges that the students — one of whom had been disciplined by Draker — created the page to get revenge, and that it was designed to "injure Ms. Draker's reputation, expose her to public hatred ... and cause her harm." The suit also alleges that the youths' parents were grossly negligent in supervising them.

- Ligonier Ministries, a religious broadcaster and publisher in Lake Mary, Fla., has taken the unusual step of asking a judge to pre-emptively silence a blogger to try to prevent him from criticizing the ministries. Judges historically have refused to place such limits on traditional publishers.

The lawsuit cites postings on a blog by Frank Vance that described Ligonier president Timothy Dick as "a shark" and as coming from a "family of nincompoops." The suit says the entries are false and have damaged Dick's reputation.

Robert Cox, founder and president of the Media Bloggers Association, which has 1,000 members, says the recent wave of lawsuits means that bloggers should bone up on libel law. "It hasn't happened yet, but soon, there will be a blogger who is successfully sued and who loses his home," he says. "That will be the shot heard round the blogosphere."

Wild West of the Internet

At its best, the blogosphere represents the ultimate in free speech by giving voice to millions. It is the Internet's version of Speaker's Corner in London's Hyde Park, a global coffeehouse where ideas are debated and exchanged.

The blogosphere also is the Internet's Wild West, a rapidly expanding frontier town with no sheriff. It's a place where both truth and "truthiness" thrive, to use the satirical word coined by comedian Stephen Colbert as a jab at politicians for whom facts don't matter.

Nearly two blogs are created every second, according to Technorati, a San Francisco firm that tracks more than 53 million blogs. Besides forming online communities in which people share ideas, news and gossip and debate issues of the day, blogs empower character assassins and mischief makers.

Small disputes now can lead to huge embarrassment, thanks to websites such as bitterwaitress.com, which purports to identify restaurant patrons who leave miserly tips. DontDateHimGirl.com includes postings that have identified men as pedophiles, rapists and diseased, without verification the postings are true.

"People take advantage of the anonymity to say things in public they would never say to anyone face-to-face," Cox says. "That's where you get these horrible comments. This is standard operating procedure."

Even so, Cox thinks the chief danger in legal disputes over what's said on the Internet is the potential chilling effect it could have on free speech. Many lawsuits against bloggers, he says, are filed merely to silence critics. In those cases, he encourages bloggers to fight back.

Last April, Cox orchestrated an effective counterattack on behalf of a blogger in Maine who was sued by a New York ad agency for $1 million. Lance Dutson, a website designer, had been blogging for two years when he posted several essays accusing Maine's Department of Tourism of wasting taxpayers' money. Among other things, he posted a draft of a tourism ad that mistakenly had contained a toll-free number to a phone-sex line.

Warren Kremer Paino Advertising, which produced the tourism campaign, said in its suit that Dutson made defamatory statements "designed to blacken WKPA's reputation (and) expose WKPA to public contempt and ridicule."

Dutson's criticisms paled to those directed at WKPA after word of the lawsuit spread through the blogosphere. Bloggers rushed to defend Dutson, and several lawyers volunteered to represent him. The media picked up the story and cast it as David vs. Goliath. Eight days after filing the suit, WKPA dropped it without comment.

"We're not here to play nice with somebody who is trying to suppress the speech of one of my members," Cox says.

Who should be sued?

A key principle that courts use in determining whether someone has been libeled is what damage the offending article did to that person's reputation in his or her community.

Susan Crawford, a professor at Cardoza Law School in New York who specializes in media and Internet issues, says the ease with which false postings can be corrected instantly, among other things, will force judges to reconsider how to measure the damage that is done to a plaintiff's reputation.

"Libel law depends on having a reputation in a particular town that's damaged," she says. "Do you have an online reputation? What's your community that hears about the damage to your online reputation? Who should be sued? The original poster? Or someone like the Wonkette, for making something really famous? The causes of action won't go away. But judges will be skeptical that a single, four-line (posting in a) blog has actually damaged anyone."

Greg Herbert, an Orlando lawyer who represented Dutson, disagrees. The principles of libel law aren't going to change, he says. However, some judges "might not think a blogger is entitled to the same sort of free speech protection others are. A lot of judges still don't know what a blog is, and they think the Internet is a dark and nefarious place where all kinds of evil deeds occur."

Judges have indicated that they will give wide latitude to the type of speech being posted on the Internet. They usually have cited the 1996 Communications Decency Act, which protects website owners from being held liable for postings by others. On the other hand, under that statute, individuals who post messages are responsible for their content and can be sued for libel. That applies whether they are posting on their own website or on others' message boards.

In May, a federal judge in Philadelphia cited the act in dismissing a lawsuit stemming from a series of postings on a website operated by Tucker Max, a Duke Law School graduate whose site features tales of his boozing and womanizing.

Posters on a message board on tuckermax.com had ridiculed Anthony DiMeo III, the heir to a New Jersey blueberry farm fortune, accusing him of inflating his credentials as a publicist, event planner and actor. DiMeo sued Max last March, claiming in court papers that his manhood had been questioned, his professional skills lampooned and his social connections mocked. DiMeo said Max, through the website, had libeled and threatened him, noting that one poster had written: "I can't believe no one has killed (DiMeo) yet."

In dismissing the suit, U.S. District Judge Steward Dalzell noted that Max "could be a poster child for the vulgarity" on the Internet, but that he nevertheless was entitled to protection under the Communications Decency Act. After the decision, DiMeo ridiculers on tuckermax.com piled on. Max says more than 200,000 people have viewed various threads on his message board about DiMeo.

DiMeo has asked an appeals court to consider not only the original messages about him but also those posted since the court decision. Alan Nochumson, DiMeo's attorney, says the criticism has amounted to an Internet gang attack, led by Max, that has significantly damaged DiMeo's business. Nochumson says when Internet users use Google to search for DiMeo's name, many of the first web links that pop up direct readers to postings on Max's website that criticize DiMeo.

Max says the claim is absurd. "The Internet isn't some giant ant colony," he says. "Different people from all over the country do things. I don't control them."

Third-party comments

Hollis' lawsuit against DontDateHimGirl.com could reveal how far courts are willing to go to protect website owners from third-party comments. His suit claims the site is not the equivalent of an Internet provider such as AOL or Yahoo, and that because Joseph edits the site, she should be liable for its contents.

Hollis has sued Joseph, a Miami publicist and former *Miami Herald* columnist, as well as seven women who posted the messages about him. Three are named in the suit; four are anonymous.

Joseph's attorney, Lida Rodriguez-Taseff, says Joseph does not edit postings, except to remove information such as Social Security numbers and addresses.

"If a court were to find that the Communications Decency Act doesn't apply to Tasha, no website would be safe," Rodriguez-Taseff says, adding that if courts start to hold website owners liable for the content of third-party postings, "the only people who would be able to provide forums (would be) wealthy people. ... It would be like making the coffee shop owner responsible for what people say in his coffee shop. What this case would say is that providers of forums in the Internet would have an obligation to determine truth or falsity of posts."

A hearing is scheduled Oct. 19. "The Internet has a great number of valuable tools with which people can do great things," Hollis says.

But he says he's disturbed by how such false personal information can spread so freely across the web. "Even if I had herpes, which I don't, even if I was gay, which I'm not, would I want to have a conversation about those things with an anonymous individual over a global platform? It's utterly ridiculous."

Even if he wins in court, Hollis says, he loses.

"Those postings are going to be out there forever," he says. "Whenever anybody Googles my name, up comes a billion sites. I will forever have to explain to someone that I do not have herpes."

Basic defense for libel: The truth

In Cumming, Ga., about 40 miles northeast of Atlanta, David Milum, 58, is still blogging. He is appealing the $50,000 judgment against him.

Milum says he considers himself a muckraker and exposer of corruption in local officials. In the recent libel trial, his attorney, Jeff Butler, described his client a "rabble-rouser" whose inspiration was "public service."

Milum lost in court because he could not meet the basic defense for libel claims: He could not prove that his allegations that Banks was involved in bribery and corruption were true.

Now Milum is facing another libel suit — this one seeking $2 million — over his claims about the alleged misdeeds of a local government employee.

"I have a very wonderful wife," Milum says. "And you can imagine how wonderful she has to be to put up with this."

Things to Think About

1. What group tracks Internet litigation in the United States? How are blogs targeted? Why?

2. How has the legal mindset of bloggers changed? Why is this surprising?

3. Is there an ethical dilemma involved in posting a negative statement about another individual over the Internet? How would this violate the Golden Rule?

4. What does Cox feel is the chief danger in these legal disputes? Argue for both sides of the controversy. Provide evidence.

5. A key principle that courts use in determining whether someone has been libeled is assessment of damage to that person's reputation. What will be the legal issues that surround this principle?

Key Terms

1. Libel

2. Communications Decency Act